# Maize Craze

## Spectacular Sweet Corn Recipes

**Marie Porter**

Photography by
Michael Porter

www.celebrationgeneration.com

# Maize Craze



Second Edition, July 2019
(Originally "Sweet Corn Spectacular", published by Minnesota Historical
Society Press)

I.S.B.N. 978-0-9976608-6-9

Published and Distributed by

Marie Porter
P.O. Box 36583, Eastgate PO
Hamilton, ON
L8E5B2

**www.celebrationgeneration.com**

*Cover Photos, Clockwise from Top Left:*

*Breakfast Corn Muffins , page 21*
*White Chocolate Sweet Corn Truffles , page 150*
*Roasted Corn Chowder, page 78*
*Sweet Corn Panna Cotta , page 132*
*Sweet Corn Bruschetta , page 66*

*Back Cover Photo:*

*Atol de Elote, page 116*

# Acknowledgments

As always, major props to my husband, Michael Porter... The King of All Corn Freaks.

As with all of my books, he has contributed gorgeous photography, recipe testing, and constant, unwavering support for the project.

This time around has been even more hands-on for him, as it was his love for - well, let's be honest... obsession with! - corn that inspired this project, leading up to the original publication of "Sweet Corn Spectacular", way back in 2013!

Additionally, my sincerest thanks go out to everyone who contributed to the Maize Craze Kickstarter project financially, and also to those who spread the word and encouraged others to have a look at the campaign. I hope you love the result of your generosity!

This was my fifth cookbook project to come to fruition as the result of a crowd funding campaign, and many of you have been with me since the first, Beyond Flour. I appreciate all of your support!

Additionally, I would like to think DeBackere Farms Inc, Josmar Acres and Snyder's Sweet Corn for their assistance in getting the word out.

# Table of Contents

# Foreword

As a child, corn was an integral part of our diet - sometimes canned, sometimes creamed, sometimes fresh on the cob.  It was so ubiquitous, that I never really gave much thought to it ... if that makes sense.

As time passed, I came to learn the beauty of a perfect ear of fresh sweet corn. Growing up in Manitoba, the Morden Corn and Apple Festival was a big deal - and the corn there was so much plumper and sweeter than anything that came frozen or in a can. Those golden ears of corn were something to look forward to throughout the year... and then gorge ourselves silly on, when the time was right!

I grew up, left my hometown and moved out east - and the corn was never the same. The sweetness of that prairie corn just wasn't there. Instead of fresh from the farm, the commonly available corn had been trucked in, and had gone starchy. Who knew corn could change in quality so quickly? It was back to canned and frozen, for me.

Eventually, I moved to Minnesota and married the King of All Corn Freaks.

Like me, he had been raised on corn. Canned corn was a regular part of his diet, and every summer, his family made a point of picking up fresh corn on the side of the road, en route to their cabin.

UNLIKE me, he was perfectly ok with making meals out of nothing but corn. In his mind, why would he need anything else, if he had a can of creamed corn on hand? That was his bliss.

Yes, while I enjoyed corn, he could survive on it.  Seriously.  While many people will joke that they could live on a particular food... he really would be perfectly happy with nothing but corn based meals for the rest of his life.

Early on in our relationship, I decided to put his love of corn to the test, and so began "The Day of Corn". For his birthday one year, all of his meals and snacks were corn based.  We had corn pancakes for breakfast, corn salsa and corn ships as a snack, a cornmeal bake for lunch, corn burgers for supper... even corn ice cream, for dessert.

He loved it.   So began a tradition in our house: coming up with all kinds of new and interesting ways to cook with corn... and - eventually - this book.

While you and yours may not share the degree of his obsession with it, I'm sure you'll love the result of it.

I think that many of us can fall into the rut of "boiled or grilled?" when it comes to fresh corn on the cob.  Before developing this book, I know that I certainly did!

Corn is especially interesting to work with, as you can use it as a grain or a vegetable, and you can also use its sweetness as a base for desserts.  Extremely versatile!

We had a lot of fun developing these recipes, as well as some that didn't made it into the book.  I hope that you have fun perusing the book, and tasting the many interesting ways that fresh corn can be used!

*- Marie*

# Corn: The Basics

## What is Corn?

Corn belongs to the genus *Zea* - which is a genus of grasses in the family *Poaceae*. Contrary to its popular home-cooking use as a vegetable, corn is a grain.  Not just any grain, mind you.  Corn is known as America's first grain, having been cultivated over 6,000 years ago.

Corn cultivation began in Mesoamerica, as a domesticated variety of teosinte - an ancient grass. Popular cultivation of corn spread outward from there, throughout a large portion of what is now North America, as well as the northern parts of what is now South America.

Sometime in the late fifteeth or early sixteenth century, corn made its way across the Atlantic ocean, likely on Columbus's first or second trip home. Landing in Europe, corn soon made its way across Northern Africa and Asia.

The earliest cultivars of corn didn't look or taste anything like the corn of today - they had small kernels, spaced further apart, and were far more starchy. Over thousands of years, corn has been cultivated to be larger, with plumper and more numerous kernels.  Corn destined for eating as-is (rather than being milled or otherwise processed) was developed to be much sweeter than earlier - or more industrial - counterparts.

Nowadays, corn is the third largest grain crop in Canada - number one in Ontario - and is used for fuel and in some plastic production, in addition to its use as a fresh food and processed grain product. Additionally, it's the most produced cereal grain crop in the world.

# Selecting, Handling and Storing Corn

Corn is a relatively finicky "vegetable" (again, it's a grain!), losing its oomph pretty quickly after being picked.  Once picked, the sugars in corn begin converting to starch.  As this happens, the sweetness diminishes and the corn begins to taste mealy - not at all the tender, sweet kernels that you get from a fresher ear of corn.

Of course, corn should be eaten while it's as fresh as possible... but how do you determine "Fresh"?  Look for silk that is only just beginning to turn brown, and for a pale green stem.  Stems that are white or brown, or even yellowed are past their prime.  Ears should have fresh, healthy looking husks - don't buy them if the husks have dried out. The ear should have a good sized diameter, not be long and skinny. Upon peeling back the husk, you will want kernels that are fat and firm, shiny, and free of any bugs, mold, or rot.

When purchasing corn from the grocery store or farmer's market, resist the urge to shuck it right on the spot. Leaving the husks on protects the corn and keep it moist, preserving its freshness. Keep your ears of corn - husks and all - in your fridge until you're ready to cook them.

Right before cooking your corn, you'll need to shuck it. Peel back the husk - the green, leafy portion of the corn - and snap off any remaining portion of the stalk.

While the kernels, cob, and even the husk have their uses, you'll definitely want to get rid of the corn silk that clings to the cob. Use a damp paper towel to quickly and easily remove the threads - just wipe it down in a straight line motion, starting at the tip, heading towards the stalk.

When it comes to storing, just remember that corn will lose its sweetness very fast - always try to use corn within a couple days of purchase.  Wrap corn - still in its husk - in damp paper towels, and refrigerate in a plastic bag.

# Cooking with Corn

Before getting to all of the wonderful and unique things you can cook with corn, let's address the basic preparations.  Sometimes, you just want a perfectly cooked ear of corn on the cob!

**Boiling**

Boiling is probably the most popular preparation of fresh corn on the cob, for good reason: It's quick, easy, and - when done right - produces really tasty results.

The key to properly boiling corn is to not over cook it.  Fresh corn kernels contain a "milk" - when overcooked, this liquid firms up, and the corn becomes tough. You're aiming more to just heat it, rather than actually cook it.

For corn that is nice and fresh, bring a pot of water to a boil, then add your shucked ears of corn.  Allow to cook for 3 minutes, and remove.

For corn that may be a little past it's prime, add a bit of milk - about ½ cup - to your boiling water, along with a couple tablespoons of sugar.  This will help bring the corn back to a sweeter taste when served.

Milk and sugar are not only unnecessary when preparing very fresh corn, they're undesirable - you don't want to mask the great flavour of perfectly fresh corn on the cob.

The thing that you never want to do when boiling corn on the cob is to salt the water.  This toughens the kernel as it draws moisture from the corn.  Not cool!

You're free to salt the corn - whether from salted butter, or by sprinkling salt directly onto the cob - as you're ready to eat it!


**Steaming**

If you have a steamer, this can be another attractive option for cooking corn. Simply cover the bottom of your steamer with a few inches of water, and arrange your shucked ears of corn on the steamer's rack.  Steam for 5-10 minutes, or until just heated through.

**Microwaving**

Some people enjoy microwaving their corn, preferring the ease and speed to all other methods. It's all good!  There are two main ways of nuking corn on the cob, both of which end up amounting to a steaming method:

First of all, you can microwave the corn right in the husk. The husk keeps the moisture in as the cob is heated, essentially steaming it right there in it's own casing.  To do this, place your unshucked cob in the microwave and heat it on high for 2-3 minutes.

Alternatively, you can steam your shucked corn in a glass bowl.  Add a couple inches of water to the bottom of a glass cooking dish, then arrange your already-shucked ears of corn in the bowl.  Cover with plastic wrap, cut a few slits in it, and microwave for 4-6 minutes.  Once the time is up, carefully remove the plastic wrap - while the slits were put in the plastic to allow steam to escape, there will still be a fair amount of steam remaining in the bowl. Don't burn yourself!

**Oven Roasting**

Cooking your corn in the oven is a great way to impart a bit of a "roasty" flavour to your ears of corn.   Place corn - still in the husk - directly on the oven rack and roast for 30 minutes at 350F.  Much like microwaving, this also steams the cob within its casing.

**Smoking Corn on the Cob**

Have a smoker?  You can use it for more than just meat - smoked corn on the cob is fabulous!  To smoke corn on the cob, you'll want to remove the corn silk.  So, pull the outer husk down, but not all the way OFF the corn. Remove the silk, and soak the de-silked ear of corn in a bucket of cold water for at least an hour, preferably 2+ hours.

Prepare a fire in your smoker, using whatever flavour wood chips you would like. We tend to use hickory chips, and preheat the temp to 325°F.

Place cobs into your smoker, leaving space around each. Allow to smoke for 15-30 minutes or so, then remove from smoker. 15 minutes results in a lightly cooked corn cob, smoking for longer will cook the corn more and impart more smoke flavour.

Carefully peel back the husk of each cob of corn, brush with butter (Try a compound butter, page 107), and replace the husk once more.  Return cobs to the smoker, and allow to smoke for another 30-45 minutes, or until done. Serve with more butter.

**Grilling**

Grilling has long been a favorite way of cooking food during the summer months, and it's a great way to prepare corn on the cob. More than any other preparation, it seems that everyone has their own favorite method of doing this.  As it's largely a matter of preference, I highly encourage you to experiment and see what you like best!  A few techniques:

- Shuck the corn, grill on indirect heat for 8-10 minutes.

- Shuck the corn, heat in boiling water for 2 minutes, then grill on direct heat just until grill marks form.

- Peel back the husk of the corn, remove corn silk.  Apply butter to the cob, replace the husk (encasing the butter).  Grill for a few minutes on direct heat.  If you like your corn a little charred, remove a bit of the husk before grilling - just not enough to allow the butter to escape!

- Completely shuck the corn, dip it in water, grill for a few minutes on direct heat.

- Soak a few tooth picks in water for at least 30 minutes.  Wrap shucked corn in strips of bacon (1.5 - 2 strips per cob), secure ends of bacon with soaked tooth picks.  Grill until bacon is cooked.

- Soak shucked ears or corn in a mixture of half buttermilk, half water for an hour or two, then grill over direct heat for a few minutes.

**Bacon Wrapped Corn on the Cob**

This is such a simple way to prepare corn on the cob - there's not really anything elegant about it - but it's such a tasty preparation!  The bacon adds flavour, salt, and fat to the corn as it roasts, basting the corn in wonderful deliciousness.

4 ears sweet corn, husks removed
8 slices of bacon (regular, not thick cut)
Pepper and salt (optional)

Wrap 2 slices of bacon around each ear of corn, securing with toothpicks. Arrange on a broiling pan, sprinkle with ground pepper.

Set broiler to high, broil for 6-8 minutes.  Remove from oven, flip cobs over, continue broiling for another 4-5 or until bacon is desired doneness. Salt to taste, if desired - the bacon provides salt, so it's entirely optional.

*Grilled Corn*

**Eat it Raw!**

If you're lucky enough to get your hands on some peak-season, perfectly fresh corn... try eating it raw!  Not really advisable for off season or starchy corn, this is a special treat!


**Freezing Fresh Corn**

Have you found yourself with more perfectly sweet, fresh corn on the cob than you can possibly eat in the next two days?  Freeze some of it!

Get a large pot of water boiling, and remove the husks from your corn.  Blanch whole cobs of corn at a full rolling boil for about 5 minutes. Once cobs have been cooked at a full rolling boil for 5 minutes, remove from boiling water and plunge into ice cold water immediately, to stop the cooking process. Allow to sit in the ice water for another 5 minutes, and then drain.

Use a sharp knife to cut the kernels from each cooled cob of corn, spread in a single layer on a cookie sheet lined with parchment paper. Freeze for one hour. (You can skip this if you don't need the kernels individually frozen)

Bag your frozen kernels into good quality freezer bags, or - better yet - vacuum sealed bags. Remove as much air as you can, label with the date, and freeze.

*Hot Fresh Corn "Cereal"*

# Breakfast & Brunch

## Hot Fresh Corn "Cereal"

When I was young, one of my favorite breakfast foods was sliced bananas in milk, with sugar. It was incredibly simple, but so good!

Now - being married to the biggest corn freak in the world - I wanted to do a corn version for my husband. I tweaked it a bit to really focus on the best qualities of the corn. It's now a warm dish, with the sweetness incorporated into the liquid rather than sprinkled on top. The milk has been swapped out for coconut milk, making the dish feel more breakfast-y. A bit of cornstarch thickens the mixture, really driving home the feeling of comfort food.

Coconut milk, a creamy liquid, is usually sold in the Asian foods aisle. It is not to be confused with creamed coconut, which is much, much thicker.

Serves 2

| | | |
|---|---|---|
| Ears fresh sweet corn, husks removed | 3–4 | 3-4 |
| 1 Can coconut milk | 14 oz | 400 ml |
| Granulated sugar | 2 Tbsp | 30 ml |
| Cold water | 2 Tbsp | 30 ml |
| Cornstarch | 1 Tbsp | 15 ml |
| Vanilla extract | ½ tsp | 2 ml |
| Salt | | |

Using a sharp knife, carefully cut kernels off the ears of corn.

Add kernels to a medium saucepan, along with coconut milk, sugar, water, and cornstarch. Whisk well to combine; cook over medium heat until warmed though, and mixture thickens.

Once thickened, remove from heat.  Stir in vanilla, season with salt to taste.  Serve hot, garnished with fresh fruit, if desired.

*Breakfast Corn Muffins*

# Breakfast Corn Muffins

Corn is such a versatile ingredient, the possibilities for these muffins are endless! While I'm providing a few suggestions, feel free to run with it!  Makes 12 muffins

| | | |
|---|---|---|
| All-purpose flour | 1 ½ cups | 375 ml |
| Yellow cornmeal | 3/4 cup | 175 ml |
| Baking powder | 1 tsp | 5 ml |
| Salt | ½ tsp | 2 ml |
| Butter, softened | ½ cup | 125 ml |
| Granulated sugar | 2/3 cup | 150 ml |
| Liquid honey | 2 Tbsp | 30 ml |
| Large eggs | 2 | 2 |
| Milk | 2/3 cup | 150 ml |
| Ears fresh sweet corn, husks removed | 2 | 2 |

Preheat oven to 400 F (200 C).  Prepare muffin pan with cupcake/muffin cups, or grease well.  Combine flour, cornmeal, baking powder and salt, stirring until well combined.  Set aside.

In a large bowl, cream together butter, sugar, and honey until light and fluffy.  Add in eggs and milk, carefully stir until well incorporated. Mix in the dry ingredients, stirring just until combined. Using a sharp knife, carefully cut kernels off the ears of corn.  Stir corn into batter, just until distributed.   Spoon batter into prepared muffin pan.  Bake for 22-25 minutes, until a knife or toothpick inserted into the center of a muffin comes out clean.

*Blueberry:*      Add 1 cup of fresh blueberries along with the corn kernels.

*Peanut Butter Banana:*   Decrease sugar to ½ cup.  Add ½ cup peanut butter when creaming the butter and sugar together, and 1 chopped banana with the corn kernels.

*Jalapeno, Bacon, Cheese -*      Decrease sugar to 1/4 cup. Add 1 finely chopped jalapeno, 6 slices of crispy bacon (crumbled), and 1 cup of shredded sharp cheddar cheese along with the corn kernels

*Sausage:*      Decrease sugar to 1/4 cup. Add 1 cup of crumbled or sliced cooked breakfast sausage, 1/4 cup finely chopped onion, and 1 cup of shredded cheese along with the corn kernels

Sour Cream & Onion:     Decrease sugar to 1/3 cup, decrease milk to 1/4 cup, add
½ cup sour cream with the milk and eggs.  Add ½ cup
finely sliced green onions with the corn kernels. (This is
also great with bacon!)

# Sweet Corn Pancakes

I created this recipe for my husband's first "day of corn" breakfast, and it was a
huge hit!  While there are many recipes which use straight up canned corn kernels,
I wanted the corn flavour to permeate the batter itself - this recipe involves a little
more effort than others, but is well worth it.   As with many pancake recipes, this
also works well in a waffle maker. For a savoury pancake, decrease the sugar to 1
Tbsp, serve with salsa and sour cream.

Makes about 4 servings

| | | |
|---|---|---|
| Ears fresh sweet corn, husks removed | 3 | 3 |
| Buttermilk* | 3/4 cup | 175 ml |
| Large eggs | 2 | 2 |
| Butter, melted | 1/4 cup | 50 ml |
| All purpose flour | 1 cup | 250 ml |
| Granulated sugar | 2-3 Tbsp | 30-45 ml |
| Baking powder | 1 Tbsp | 15 ml |
| Salt | ½ tsp | 2 ml |

Using a sharp knife, carefully cut kernels off the ears of corn.  Use the side of a fork
to scrape any remaining corn kernel bits / milk / pulp off the stripped cobs, into a
blender. Add a large handful of the kernels to the blender, reserving the rest. Add
buttermilk, blend until smooth. Add egg and melted butter, blitz for a few seconds
until well combined.

In a large bowl, combine flour, sugar, baking powder, and salt. Add remaining corn
kernels, as well as the blended wet ingredients. Gently stir, just until combined.

Lightly oil your griddle or frying pan, preheat over medium or medium-low heat.
Scoop 1/4 cup amounts of batter onto the griddle. Gently spread batter out into a
larger circle, about 4 – 4.5" in diameter. Cook until bubbles start popping through
top surface. Flip, cook until done.  Serve with maple syrup, whipped cream, and/or
blueberries.

*If you don't have buttermilk, use 3/4 milk, with 1 ½ tsp lemon juice mixed in.

*Sweet Corn Pancakes*

# Buttermilk Corn Scones

As with many of the recipes in this book, this scone recipe is a solid base - crusty on the outside, tender on the inside - with room for endless customization. You can go sweet or savoury with the additions, and really just include almost anything you want!  These are not overly sweet to start, so if you're looking to make them a more desserty breakfast or snack, you may want to increase the sugar to 1/3-1/2 cup.

Makes 8

| All purpose flour | 2 cups | 500 ml |
| Cornmeal | ½ cup | 125 ml |
| Granulated sugar | 1/4 cup | 50 ml |
| Baking powder | 2 tsp | 10 ml |
| Salt | 1 1/4 tsp | 6 ml |
| Unsalted butter, chilled | 6 Tbsp | 90 ml |
| Ear fresh sweet corn, husk removed | 1 | 1 |
| Buttermilk* | 1 cup | 250 ml |

Preheat oven to 400 F (200 C).  Line baking sheet with parchment paper.

In a large bowl, combine flour, cornmeal, sugar, baking powder and salt. Chop chilled butter into small cubes. Cut butter into dry ingredients using a fork (or two!) or a pastry blender / cutter until mixture is distributed throughout, and mixture resembles gravel.

Using a sharp knife, carefully cut kernels off the ears of corn.  Add corn and buttermilk to dry ingredients, stir JUST until combined - mixture will be a little sticky.  Turn dough out onto a floured surface, sprinkling some flour on top. Gently knead for a few seconds, then gather dough up into a ball.  Press down to an even 1" thickness, cut into 8 wedges.  Transfer scones to prepared baking sheet, bake for about 25 minutes or until golden brown.

*If not buttermilk, use 1 cup milk, with 1 tbsp lemon juice mixed in.

**Variations:**

- Add 1 cup shredded cheddar & 1-2 finely chopped jalapenos with the corn kernels
- Add 2/3 cup fresh blueberries with the corn kernels
- Add 2/3 cup sweetened dried cranberries with the corn kernels
- Add zest of one orange with the corn kernels (also works well with dried cranberries!)

*Buttermilk Corn Scones*

# Grilled Corn and Pepper Hash with Ham and Eggs

This recipe is great done up the morning after a grilled dinner.  Toss an extra couple ears of corn and the peppers on the grill along with supper one night, use them as leftovers the next morning!   Also great as a camping meal, any time of the day.

If you're unable to find poblano peppers, feel free to substitute green bell, banana, or any other mild-medium type pepper of your choice.

We like to use a hickory smoked ham for this, but feel free to use whatever variety you want - even vegetarian varieties work well with this!

Serves 4

| | | |
|---|---|---|
| Red bell pepper | 1 | 1 |
| Poblano pepper | 1 | 1 |
| Small red onion | 1 | 1 |
| Ears fresh sweet corn, husks removed | 2 | 2 |
| Olive oil | 1/4 cup | 50 ml |
| Butter | 1 Tbsp | 15 ml |
| Diced smoked ham | 2 cups | 500 ml |
| Garlic clove, pressed or minced | 1 | 1 |
| Salt and pepper | | |
| Large eggs | 4 | 4 |

Slice red and poblano peppers into large flat pieces, and onion into 1/2" thick slices. Brush peppers, onion, and corn cobs with olive oil.  Grill or broil everything until as "done" as you would like - personally, I like some dark grill marks for this, but not an overall char. Remove items as they are ready - the peppers will cook the fastest. Allow everything to cool enough to handle.

Chop up the peppers and onion, use a sharp knife to remove kernels from the corn, set aside.

Heat butter in a large frying pan, add ham and garlic.  Cook over medium for two minutes, until ham is warmed through. Add chopped peppers, onion, and corn, stir well, season with salt and pepper to taste.

Arrange 4 little "wells" in your fry pan ingredients. Crack an egg into each, sprinkle with a little salt and pepper, cover pan, and cook until eggs reach desired doneness. Serve hot.

*Grilled Corn and Pepper Hash with Ham and Eggs*

# "Corned" Beef Hash

What started out as an attempt at being "punny" actually produced a very balanced, delicious breakfast.  The sweetness of the corn is the perfect complement to the saltiness of the corned beef.

If you're making this with leftovers from a  Corned Beef dinner, feel free to use leftover potatoes that were cooked in with the brisket - it's easier and brings extra flavour!

| | | |
|---|---|---|
| Red potatoes | 1 lb | 500 g |
| Olive oil | 2 Tbsp | 30 ml |
| Large green pepper, chopped | 1 | 1 |
| Small onion, chopped | 1 | 1 |
| Ears fresh sweet corn, husk removed | 2 | 2 |
| Cooked corned beef brisket | 1 lb | 500 g |
| Chopped parsley | 1/4 cup | 50 ml |
| Salt and pepper | | |

Chop potatoes into ½" cubes, boil until just tender. Drain well, set aside.

In a large skillet, saute olive oil, green pepper, and onion until vegetables are tender. Add potatoes, continue to cook until potatoes are browned.

Using a sharp knife, carefully cut kernels off the ears of corn.  Remove any extra fat from corned beef, chop or shred it into bite sized pieces.

Add corn kernels to pan, along with corned beef. Continue cooking until corned beef is heated through.  Add parsley, stir well, and season with salt and pepper to taste.

Serve hot - this goes particularly well served with a fried egg on top!

*"Corned" Beef Hash*

# Corn Frittata

The beauty of frittatas are that you can really put whatever you like in them. This recipe is for a very basic version of a corn frittata - have fun with it!  Add bacon, vegetables, your choice of herbs and spices... whatever you want. Also, feel free to add seasonings to this base recipe. Depending on your choice of add ins, various fresh or dried herbs and spices will work well.  Traditionally, this is made with a nonstick, cast iron skillet.  Personally, I don't like using cast iron at all (don't judge!), so I just make this in a glass baking dish.  I've written this recipe in the traditional technique, but if you're like me... pour the mixture into a greased glass baking dish, and bake for 30-40 minutes, or until set. There's no need for the additional stove top cooking when you're using a glass dish.  Serves 4-6

| Large eggs | 8 | 8 |
| --- | --- | --- |
| Milk | 1/4 cup | 50 ml |
| Garlic cloves , pressed or minced | 1-2 | 1-2 |
| Ears fresh sweet corn, husks removed | 2-3 | 2-3 |
| Small onion, finely chopped | 1 | 1 |
| Add ins* | 2 cups | 500 ml |
| Olive oil | 2 Tbsp | 300 ml |
| Salt and pepper | | |
| Shredded cheese of choice | ½ - 1 cup | 125-250 ml |

Preheat oven to 400 F (200 C).  In a large bowl, whisk together eggs, milk, and garlic.  Set aside

Using a sharp knife, carefully cut kernels off the ears of corn.  Add to a large, oven proof skillet, along with onion, add-ins, and 1 Tbsp olive oil.   Saute until onions - and add ins, as applicable - are tender. Season with salt and pepper to taste. Remove from heat and allow to cool slightly.

Pour cooled saute mix into the egg mixture along with the cheese, stirring to coat. Wipe out skillet, add remaining olive oil. Pour egg and vegetable mixture back into the skillet, cook over medium heat 2 two minutes without stirring.  Turn heat down to low, cover pan with a lid, and continue to cook for another 2 minutes.  Remove the lid, transfer skillet to top shelf of the oven.  Bake until entire frittata is set, and the top is golden brown.  Cut into wedges and serve warm.

* Mix and match any of the following, in whatever proportions you like:  Chopped red or green pepper (saute before adding), zucchini, mushrooms, broccoli, cilantro, parsley, green onions, leftover potatoes (Cooked and chopped), fresh basil, cooked chicken (chopped), breakfast sausage chunks, bacon.

*Corn Frittata*

# Corn, Kale, and Bacon Strata

This is my favorite flavour combination for a breakfast strata, but it's definitely open to tinkering and interpretation. Stratas are easy to adapt, and a great way to use up whatever odds and ends you may have in your fridge. Swap out the kale for spinach, or for a cup or so of your favorite veggie. Use your favorite cheese, add your favorite herbs and spices if you'd like. I like to use crusty, day old baguette to make the strata, but it can also work with your favorite sour dough, French, Italian, or random artisan type breads - just leave them out to dry out a bit overnight, and cut into 1" cubes. You'll want about 8 cups of bread cubes, whatever type you use. Serves 4-6

| | | |
|---|---|---|
| Ears fresh sweet corn, husks removed | 2 | 2 |
| Large onion, finely chopped | 1 | 1 |
| Bacon slices, chopped | 6 | 6 |
| Bunch of kale, chopped | 1 | 1 |
| Salt | ½ tsp | 2 ml |
| Black pepper | ½ tsp | 2 ml |
| Large eggs | 9 | 9 |
| Dijon mustard | 1-2 Tbsp | 15-30 ml |
| Milk | 2 2/3 cups | 650 ml |
| Cooking spray or butter | | |
| Baguette, cut into 1" cubes | 1 | 1 |
| Grated Swiss or Jarlsburg cheese | 2 ½ cups | 625 ml |

Using a sharp knife, carefully cut kernels off the ears of corn. Set aside. In a large frying pan, cook onion and bacon together until onion is tender and bacon is cooked, but not crispy. Add kale, sautee until kale is wilted but not yet crispy. Stir in corn, season with a bit of the salt and pepper. Sautee mixture for one more minute, remove from heat.

In a medium mixing bowl, Whisk together eggs and mustard. Add milk and remaining salt/pepper, continue whisking until well combined.

Using cooking spray or butter, grease a 9'x 13" baking/cake pan. Arrange half of the bread cubes evenly in the pan, top with half of the kale mixture, then half of the cheese. Repeat layering one more time, ending with cheese on top. Pour egg mixture evenly over everything, wrap with plastic wrap, and chill for 2-4 hours.

About an hour and a half before serving: Remove strata from fridge, preheat oven to 350 F (180 C). I like to let the strata sit on the counter for 20 minutes or so, to take the chill off it. Remove plastic wrap from strata, bake for 45-50 minutes. Strata is ready when it is cooked through and golden brown on top. Serve hot!

*Corn, Kale, and Bacon Strata*

# Sweet Corn Quiche

Writing a traditional quiche recipe for a cookbook is a difficult thing for me - like many other recipes in this book, it's the kind of thing that I never make the same way twice! How do I narrow down which flavouring ingredients I want to recommend? The possibilities are *endless*!

So, here is a great combination of flavours for a corn quiche. Feel free to play with it, substituting the meats, vegetables, and cheeses with other types, if you so desire.

Serves 6

| | | |
|---|---|---|
| Ears fresh sweet corn, husks removed | 2 | 2 |
| Milk | 1 cup | 250 ml |
| Small onion | ½ | ½ |
| Large eggs | 4 | 4 |
| Salt | ½ tsp | 2 ml |
| Smoked ham, cubed | 1 cup | 250 ml |
| Finely chopped green bell peppers | 1/4 cup+ | 50 ml+ |
| Shredded Swiss cheese, divided | 3/4 cup | 175 ml |
| 1 frozen pie crust (deep dish), thawed | | |

Preheat oven to 375 F (190 C)

Using a sharp knife, carefully cut kernels off the ears of corn.  Process corn kernels and milk together in a food processor or blender until smooth.  Add onion, eggs, and salt, blitz a few seconds, until onion is finely chopped.

Sprinkle ham, green pepper, and ½ cup of the shredded cheese  over the empty pie crust, pour filling over top.

Bake 40 minutes. Sprinkle remaining 1/4 cup shredded cheese on top, continue baking until quiche is puffy and fully set, another 10 minutes or so.  Serve warm.

Variation: Feel free to swap out the veggies, cheese, and meats.  Goat cheese, red pepper, and asparagus, for instance, is an amazing combo!

*Sweet Corn Quiche*

# Easy Corn Souffle

Souffle is something that so many people don't understand. Either it's this big scary thing, or it's.. instant cornbread with stuff thrown into it. (Spoiler: that is NOT souffle!)

Never fear, here is a recipe that produces a traditional style souffle, using easier techniques.

Yes, this will fall about 45 seconds after you take it out of the oven - that's just thermodynamics, not a failing on the part of the cook!

Serves 4

| | | |
|---|---|---|
| Butter | | |
| Ears fresh sweet corn, husks removed | 3 | 3 |
| Large eggs | 7 | 7 |
| Sour cream | ½ cup | 125 ml |
| Milk | 1/4 cup | 50 ml |
| Yellow corn meal | 1/4 cup | 50 ml |
| Mustard powder | ½ - 1 tsp | 2-5ml |
| Cayenne powder | 1/4 tsp | 1 ml |
| Salt | ½ tsp | 2 ml |
| Shredded Swiss cheese | 3/4 cup | 175 ml |
| Shredded Parmesan cheese | 1/4 cup | 50 ml |
| Slices crisp bacon, crumbled (optional) | 6 | 6 |

Preheat oven to 375 F (190 C)

Use butter to grease souffle ramekins - you'll need two 16oz, or four 8oz ceramic ramekins, about 3" tall.

Using a sharp knife, carefully cut kernels off the ears of corn. Place corn in a food processor, process until finely chopped. Add eggs, sour cream, milk, cornmeal, mustard powder, cayenne, and salt, blitz for 30 seconds.

Stir in cheeses and bacon, if using. Pour into prepared ramekins, bake for 50 minutes (if using 16 oz ramekins) or 35 minutes (if using 8 oz ramekins).

Serve immediately!

*Easy Corn Souffle*

# Breakfast Burritos

Breakfast burritos are a great breakfast on the go - their self contained nature makes them really convenient to eat on the run.  As such, I like to do these up as a make-ahead breakfast for my husband. Sunday afternoon or evening, I'll whip up a batch of these, individually wrap them and have them ready to "reheat and run" on his way out the door for the rest of the week.

Makes 5 burritos

| | | |
|---|---|---|
| Ears fresh sweet corn, husks removed | 2 | 2 |
| Poblano pepper | 1 | 1 |
| Jalapeno pepper | 1 | 1 |
| Small red onion | ½ | ½ |
| Breakfast sausage of choice | 1 lb | 500 g |
| Garlic gloves, pressed or minced | 2 | 2 |
| Large eggs | 10 | 10 |
| Milk | 1/4 cup | 50 ml |
| Salt and pepper | | |
| Large flour tortillas | 5 | 5 |
| Monterrey Jack, or other cheese of choice. | | |

Cut kernels off corn, set aside.  Seed and chop the poblano and jalapeno peppers, peel and chop the onion, and set all aside with the corn kernels.

Crumble breakfast sausage into a large nonstick pan, cook until browned.  Drain off all but about 1 Tbsp of fat. (If using a low fat sausage, cook with 1 tbsp of olive oil, add 1 more Tbsp after browned)  Add corn, peppers, onion, and garlic. Continue cooking until onion is starting to go translucent, and peppers begin to soften.

In a mixing bowl, which together eggs, milk, and a little salt and pepper.  Pour egg mixture over sausage and pepper mixture, stir to incorporate.  Cook until eggs are cooked through. Remove from heat, season with salt and pepper to taste.

To serve immediately:  Warm tortillas in the microwave.  Divide hot egg mixture between tortillas.  Sprinkle shredded cheese over each, roll as a burrito, and serve immediately.  (Optional: Grill or char with a Panini press before serving!)

To make ahead for breakfasts:  Allow egg mixture to completely cool before rolling burritos.  Wrap each in plastic film, chill until use.  Burritos should be eaten within 5 days.

*Breakfast Burritos*

# Sweet Corn Fritters

Deep fried foods obviously aren't an everyday kind of breakfast... But these fritters are a colourful and fun breakfast option for the days when you are feeling up to deep frying something in the morning.  Endlessly customizable and full of flavour!

Serves 4

| | | |
|---|---|---|
| Vegetable oil for frying | | |
| All purpose flour | 1 cup | 250 ml |
| Baking powder | 1 tsp | 5 ml |
| Granulated sugar | 1 Tbsp | 15 ml |
| Salt | ½ tsp | 2 ml |
| Cayenne powder, optional | 1/4 tsp | 1 ml |
| Large eggs | 2 | 2 |
| Milk | ½ cup | 125 ml |
| Ears fresh sweet corn, husks removed | 3 | 3 |
| Add ins* | 1 cup | 250 ml |

Start heating your vegetable oil to 350 F (180 C)– you'll want at about 1" of oil in your heavy bottomed pot.

In a large bowl, mix flour, baking powder, sugar, salt, and cayenne powder.  In a separate bowl, whisk together eggs and milk until smooth.  Pour milk and egg mixture into the dry ingredients, stirring well. Using a sharp knife, carefully cut kernels off the ears of corn.  Mix corn kernels and add-ins into the batter, making sure that everything is evenly coated.

Use an ice cream scoop, measuring cup, or two spoons to carefully scoop small amounts (2-3 Tbsp- I like to use a slightly under filled 1/4 cup measure) of batter into the preheated oil. Fry in small batches for a few minutes on each side, until fritters are golden brown. Use a slotted metal spoon to transfer cooked fritters to paper towels.  Serve hot!

*** Add ins:**   Mix and match any of the following, in whatever proportions you like, just use about 1 cup total volume of your add in blend for one batch of fritters:  Chopped onions, chopped red or green pepper, cilantro, parsley, onions, green onions, shredded cheese. Have fun with it - while vegetables are traditional, you can use some crispy, crumbled bacon if you'd like!

Also, feel free to add seasonings to this base recipe. Depending on your choice of add ins, various dried herbs and spices will work well.

*Sweet Corn Fritters*

# Arepas de Choclo

This is one of those recipes that gets me a mushy, heartfelt "I looooove you!" from my husband. It's Colombian griddled sweet corn cakes... sandwiched with cheese in the middle. Basically a grilled cheese sandwich using corn instead of bread. These are popular as a breakfast food or snack item, and differ from the standard arepa with the inclusion of fresh sweet corn - most arepas use only the arepa flour.

A note on the flour: you'll want to find masarepa, a flour made from precooked cornmeal. This is different from masa harina, which is ground from dried, treated corn. While Masa harina can be easier to find, it's not that difficult to find Masarepa - I found two different brands (with one available in a choice of white or yellow, no less!) in the international foods aisle at a nearby Walmart.

Makes about 6 arepa "sandwiches"

| | | |
|---|---|---|
| Ears fresh sweet corn, husks removed | 3 | 3 |
| Milk | 1 1/4 cups | 300 ml |
| Shredded mozzarella cheese | ½ cup | 125 ml |
| Melted butter | 2 Tbsp | 30 ml |
| Masarepa | 1 ½ cups | 375 ml |
| Granulated sugar | 2 Tbsp | 30 ml |
| Salt | 1 tsp | 5 ml |
| Butter for grilling | | |
| Sliced cheese - queso fresco or mozzarella | | |

Using a sharp knife, carefully cut kernels off the ears of corn. Transfer to a blender or food processor, blitz until fairly smooth. Add milk, shredded cheese, and melted butter, blitz to combine.

In a separate bowl, combine Masarepa, sugar, and salt. Pour corn mixture into dry mixture, and stir until well combined. Allow to sit for 2 minutes, for the masarepa to absorb the moisture. You're wanting sticky dough that will hold together when balled up. Add a little more milk or masarepa flour if needed.

Heat up a nonstick pan or griddle to medium, melt some butter on it. Measure out 1/4 cup amounts of dough, and form into 4" diameter disks, using clean hands. Carefully place the arepas onto the hot surface. Cook for a few minutes, until golden on the bottom side. Gently flip - the arepas are somewhat fragile! - and cook for a few more minutes, until golden brown on the other side. Place a slice of cheese on each of half of the arepas, top each with one of the remaining arepas. Remove from heat and serve immediately.

*Arepas de Choclo*

*Beer Battered Corn on the Cob*

# Appetizers & Sides

## Beer Battered Corn on the Cob

About a decade ago, I was particularly not in the mood to brave the crowds at the Minnesota State Fair, so I made my husband a deal. I would come up with a recipe for corn on the cob IN a corn based batter and deep fry it.. if we didn't go to the Fair. Hell, I'd even do it "on a stick" to give him a bit more of the State Fair experience… but at home.  I lived up to my end of it, and we were both *very* pleasantly surprised by the results. Here's how you can make the same at home!

Serves 4

| | | |
|---|---|---|
| Ears fresh sweet corn, husks removed | 4 | 4 |
| All-purpose flour | 1 cup | 250 ml |
| Yellow cornmeal | 1 cup | 250 ml |
| Baking powder | 1 tsp | 5 ml |
| Salt | 1 tsp | 5 ml |
| Beer of your choice | 12 oz | 375 ml |
| Large egg, beaten | 1 | 1 |
| Wooden "candy apple" skewers/sticks, optional | | |

Preheat deep fryer to 375 F (190 C).

If your deep fryer is small, cut each ear of corn in half. If using sticks , carefully push the sharp end of the stick into one end of each ear of corn, far enough to be secure. Set aside.

In a large enough bowl to fit your ears of corn, mix together flour, cornmeal, baking powder, and salt. Add beer and egg, whisk until smooth.

Dip corn in batter one at a time, turning til coated. Carefully place in deep fryer, fry for 2-4 minutes, until coating is as dark as you'd like it.

Remove from fryer, and turn out onto paper towels to catch any extra oil.

Serve with Dijon mustard, or dipping sauce of your choice.

# Parched Corn

Parched corn is a very traditional "trail food". It was used as a high energy, lightweight food by Native Americans... and it was probably the predecessor to modern day corn nuts. It's also a popular food for survivalists. You start out with dried corn, which you can get via a few methods. You can dry your ears of corn whole, suspended from the ceiling of a dry basement / other room (don't do this if mice are an issue in your house!). You can do this either as whole cobs of corn or kernels, spread out on a sheet in your oven, dried on the lowest setting - and with the door open. This can take 12 or more hours, and really - I don't have the patience for that. So personally, we use a food dehydrator. The kernels aren't as whole and pretty as they are when dried on the cob, but really - this is a utilitarian food, and it's all going to taste the same!

Word of advice: prepare more fresh corn than you think is necessary, as it shrinks considerably when dried. As an example, we tend to get about 1 cup of dried kernels from 4 large ears of corn!

Whole ears of sweet corn, husks removed
Olive or corn oil, optional
Salt / Seasonings, optional

Prepare your food dehydrator, as necessary. For ours, this means cutting rounds of parchment paper to line the racks with, and poking some holes in for ventilation. If you have thin mesh liners, etc, you'll want to use them - dehydrated corn is tiny! Using a sharp knife, carefully cut kernels off the ears of corn. Loosely spread your corn kernels out on your dehydrator trays. Dehydrate for 8 hours or overnight, or until the kernels are very dark yellow and dried out - they'll still be a bit chewy.

Working in batches of 1 cup or so at a time, toast your corn kernels on your stove top. To do so, heat the kernels on medium low, stirring frequently. As the moisture in the kernels evaporates, the corn becomes "parched", and the kernels toast.

After a few minutes - when your kernels start to brown up a little, add a little oil if you would like - about 2 tsp for every 3 ears - tossing to coat well. Add seasonings if you're using them, once again tossing to coat well. Cook for another minute or so, to adhere the seasonings to the corn. Spread on paper towels to fully cool, before storing in an airtight container.

**Seasonings:** You can have a lot of fun with how you flavour your parched corn. Try your favorite dry herbs and spices, or even prepared popcorn seasonings (Not the healthiest option, but tastes great!). Try chili powder, cumin, garlic salt, ground ginger, onion salt, paprika, red pepper flakes, seasoned salt ... even brown sugar.

*Parched Corn*

# Fresh Corn Salsa

I modeled this recipe around the corn salsa at a popular chain of burrito restaurants, and it's wonderful!  A great multipurpose salsa, use it in your salads, on grilled meats, in a burrito, or just as a dip.

Makes about 4.5 cups

| | | |
|---|---|---|
| Ears fresh sweet corn, husks removed | 4 | 4 |
| Small red onion | 1 | 1 |
| Jalapeno peppers | 1-2 | 1-2 |
| Fresh cilantro | ½ - 2/3 cup | 125-150 ml |
| freshly squeezed lime juice | ½ cup | 125 ml |
| garlic clove, pressed (Optional) | 1 | 1 |
| Salt and pepper | | |

Use a sharp knife to remove kernels from the corn, place in a large bowl.

Chop onions, jalapeno(s), and cilantro. (Remove ribs and seeds from the jalapeno for a more mild salsa, if desired.) Add it all to the bowl of corn kernels, along with lime juice and garlic, if using.

Stir well, season with salt and pepper to taste.  Serve immediately, or chill for a few hours to allow the flavours to mingle.

*Fresh Corn Salsa*

# Roasted Corn & Pepper Salsa

This salsa is more "warm", than "hot", and features a wonderful roasty flavour. Slightly more labor intensive than a fresh salsa, but very much worth it!

Makes about 4 cups

| | | |
|---|---|---|
| Red bell peppers | 2 | 2 |
| Poblano pepper | 1 | 1 |
| Large onion | 1 | 1 |
| Jalapeno peppers | 1-2 | 1-2 |
| Ears fresh sweet corn, husks removed | 4 | 4 |
| Olive oil | 1/4 cup | 50 ml |
| Chipotle peppers in adobo sauce | 2-3 | 2-3 |
| Adobo sauce | 2 Tbsp | 30 ml |
| Garlic clove , pressed | 1 | 1 |
| Salt and pepper | | |

Slice red and poblano peppers into large flat pieces, and onion into ½" thick slices. Cut jalapeno(s) in half, removing ribs and seeds - if desired - for a more mild salsa. Brush peppers, onion, and corn cobs with olive oil.

Grill everything until as "done" as you would like - personally, I like some dark grill marks for this, but not an overall char. Remove items as they are ready - the peppers will cook the fastest. Allow everything to cool.

Chop up the peppers and onion, place in a bowl. Use a sharp knife to remove kernels from the corn, add to the bowl and stir well.

Finely chop chipotle peppers, add to the salsa along with the adobo sauce and pressed garlic. Stir well, season with salt and pepper to taste.

Serve this as soon as it's made, or cover and refrigerate for a day or so to let the flavours mix.

*Roasted Corn & Pepper Salsa*

# Cool Corn Dip

This recipe works up quickly, and is always a hit at any summer BBQ!

| | | |
|---|---|---|
| Ears fresh corn, husk removed | 3 | 3 |
| Green bell pepper | 1 | 1 |
| Red bell pepper | 1 | 1 |
| Jalapeno peppers | 1+ | 1+ |
| Garlic cloves, pressed | 1-2 | 1-2 |
| Green onions, thinly sliced | 3 | 3 |
| Shredded Monterey Jack cheese | 2 cups | 500 ml |
| Black pepper | ½ tsp | 2 ml |
| Salt | ½ tsp | 2 ml |
| Fresh lime juice | 1 Tbsp | 15 ml |
| Mayonnaise | 2/3 cup | 150 ml |
| Sour cream | 1 cup | 250 ml |

Using a sharp knife, carefully cut kernels off the ears of corn, place in a large bowl.

Seed and rough chop the peppers*, place into a food processor along with the garlic, and process till finely chopped. Add chopped peppers, green onions, and cheese to mixing bowl, stir to combine. Season with pepper, salt, and lime juice, toss to coat.

Add mayo and sour cream, stir until everything is well combined. Cover bowl with plastic wrap, chill for at least an hour to allow flavours to combine.

Serve with corn chips.

* Leave the jalapeno seeds in for more heat, if desired.

**Variation:**    I like to add ½ cup+ of chopped cilantro.... but I realize that not everyone is a fan of the herb!

Additionally - or alternatively - adding ½ tsp of cumin along with the cilantro gives a great tex mex flavour.

*Cool Corn Dip*

# Southwest Corn Fondue

Served with cubes of bread, chunks of vegetables, and slices of fruit, this makes a wonderful appetizer. Not in the mood for such a formal service?  Set it out with tortilla chips as a hot cheese dip!

Serves about 6

| | | |
|---|---|---|
| Ears fresh sweet corn, husks removed | 2 | 2 |
| Mexican beer (like Corona) | 1 cup | 250 ml |
| Fresh lime juice | 1 Tbsp | 15 ml |
| Red bell pepper | 1 | 1 |
| Orange bell pepper | 1 | 1 |
| Yellow bell pepper | 1 | 1 |
| Jalapeno pepper | 1 | 1 |
| Habanero pepper | 1 | 1 |
| Garlic cloves, pressed | 6 | 6 |
| Small onion | 1 | 1 |
| Shredded sharp cheddar cheese | 1 ½ lbs | 750g |
| Cornstarch | 4 tsp | 20 ml |

Using a sharp knife, carefully cut kernels off the ears of corn. Set aside.

In a medium sized saucepan, heat beer and lime juice over low-medium heat.

Seed and rough chop the peppers.  Put peppers, garlic, and onion in food processor or blender, and let it rip till finely chopped. Increase heat to medium or medium high, add pepper mixture to the beer, cook till everything is soft, and onion is translucent, about 5 minutes. Add corn, cook for one more minute.

In a large bowl, toss grated cheese with cornstarch. Add a good sized handful to the pot, and mix well till it is completely melted in. Add another big handful, and repeat until all the cheese is added, completely melted, and smooth (aside from the pepper bits, of course!)

Transfer to fondue pot if desired, and serve with cubes of bread, tortilla chips, slices of jicama, blanched broccoli, cauliflower, and asparagus, and slices of apples and pears.

*Southwest Corn Fondue*

# Scalloped Corn

This is a first for me: publishing someone else's recipe. My good friend Carrie insisted that her recipe is so addictive it must be included in this book, so here it is.

As the story goes, Carrie's former mother-in-law was very nice person but not a creative cook. One thing she was known for, however, was a scalloped corn dish based on a magazine-clipped recipe involving canned corn.

While everyone else raved, Carrie was less than impressed. Unable to resist an opportunity to show someone up (there's a reason we're friends), she quietly created her own version. She has not, however, served it to said former mother-in-law.

Serves 8–10

| | | |
|---|---|---|
| Ears fresh sweet corn, husks removed | 10 | 10 |
| Heavy cream | 1 cup | 250 ml |
| Butter, melted | ½ cup | 125 ml |
| Large eggs, beaten well | 3 | 3 |
| Crushed Club or Ritz crackers, divided | 2 cups | 500 ml |
| Shredded Parmesan cheese, divided | 2 cups | 500 ml |
| Salt and pepper | | |

Preheat oven to 350 F (180 C).

Use a sharp knife to remove kernels from the corn.

Transfer kernels to a large mixing bowl along with cream, melted butter, and beaten eggs. Stir in 1 cup of the crushed crackers and 1 cup of the Parmesan cheese. Season with salt and pepper to taste.

Pour corn mixture into a 9x13–inch baking dish and top with remaining cheese and cracker pieces. Bake for 30 minutes or until top is golden brown and inside is fluffy.

Serve hot

*Scalloped Corn*

# Creamed Corn

Why go for generic canned corn when you can easily make it at home... and load
it up with cream cheese, butter, and more cheese?

Sinful, yes, but oh so worth it!

Serves 6–8

| | | |
|---|---|---|
| Ears fresh sweet corn, husks removed | 6 | 6 |
| Heavy cream | 1 cup | 250 ml |
| Granulated sugar | 1 Tbsp | 15 ml |
| Cream cheese, softened | 4 oz | 125 g |
| Butter | 3 Tbsp | 45 ml |
| Grated Parmesan cheese | 1/3 cup | 75 ml |
| Salt | | |

Use a sharp knife to remove kernels from the corn. Place kernels in a medium pot
along with heavy cream and sugar.

Bring to a boil, reduce heat, and simmer for 5 minutes. Add in cream cheese and
butter, stirring until everything is well incorporated. Simmer for 5 more minutes.

Add Parmesan cheese, stirring until melted and mixed in.

Season with salt to taste, and serve hot.

*Creamed Corn*

# Esquites

Esquites is a creamy corn salad that is very popular in Mexico, where it's commonly sold by street vendors. The salad hits the perfect balances of sweet-salty and creamy-textured.

While cayenne powder is traditional, sometimes I like to swap it out for smoked serrano powder.

PS: If you haven't yet tried smoked serrano powder, you should! It's almost life changing!

Serves 4

| | | |
|---|---|---|
| Ears fresh sweet corn, husks removed | 4 | 4 |
| Jalapeño or serrano pepper, minced | 1 | 1 |
| Garlic clove, pressed or minced | 1 | 1 |
| Mayonnaise | 1/4 cup | 50 ml |
| Butter, at room temperature | 1/4 cup | 50 ml |
| Fresh lime juice | 1 Tbsp | 15 ml |
| Green onions, thinly sliced | 2 | 2 |
| Chopped cilantro | 1/4 cup | 50 ml |
| Cayenne | 1/4 tsp+ | 1 ml+ |
| Crumbled queso fresco | 1/3 cup | 75 ml |
| Salt | | |

Use a sharp knife to remove kernels from the corn; place kernels in a large pan along with jalapeño or serrano pepper and garlic. Cook over medium heat, stirring frequently, until corn is roasty and heated through. Remove from heat.

As corn is cooking, prepare dressing. In a large mixing bowl, mix together mayonnaise and butter. Add lime juice, green onions, cilantro, and cayenne, stirring well to combine.

Once corn is cooked, transfer hot kernels to the mixing bowl, tossing to coat. Stir in queso fresco, and season with salt to taste.

Divide mixture into 4 bowls or cups, and serve immediately.

*Esquites*

# Roasted Corn and Potato Salad

When I created this recipe, I had intended it to be a roasted take on a traditional - cold! - potato salad. As soon as the dressing was tossed on the hot potato salad, we couldn't help ourselves - we were picking at it LONG before it had a chance to cool. Oh, it was amazing - I think I actually preferred it hot, to its later, chilled incarnation!

Serves 4-6

| | | |
|---|---|---|
| Bacon, chopped | 1 lb | 500 g |
| Red potatoes | 3 lbs | 1500 g |
| Salt and pepper | | |
| Ears sweet corn, roasted or grilled | 3-4 | 3-4 |
| Stalks celery, sliced | 4 | 4 |
| Medium red onion, chopped | 1 | 1 |
| Finely chopped green onions | 1-2 Tbsp | 15-30 ml |
| Olive oil | ½ cup | 125 ml |
| Apple cider vinegar | 1/3 cup | 75 ml |
| Dijon mustard | 1 Tbsp | 15 ml |
| Garlic cloves, pressed | 2 | 2 |
| Pepper | ½ tsp | 2 ml |

Preheat oven to 400 F (200 C).

Cook bacon until crispy - set bacon aside, reserving the fat.

Chop potatoes into 3/4" - 1" chunks, toss with melted bacon fat. Spread onto a baking sheet lined with parchment paper or foil, season with salt and pepper. Roast until fork tender, about 30-35 minutes.

While potatoes are roasting, use a sharp knife to carefully cut kernels off the ears of corn. In a large bowl, mix together corn kernels, celery, red onion, green onions, and cooked bacon. Set aside.

Whisk olive oil, apple cider vinegar, mustard, garlic, and pepper together until it's all emulsified. Season with salt to taste.

When potatoes are ready, mix them into the large bowl of vegetables. Pour vinaigrette over top, tossing to coat. Serve immediately, allow to cool slightly and serve warm, or chill for later service.

*Roasted Corn and Potato Salad*

# Corn, Edamame, and Red Pepper Salad

My husband came home from a work meeting one day with a little condiment-sized tub of leftover edamame salad.

He'd never had it before, and thought that I would like it.  Well, that's what he claims, anyway.  The real story is that he wanted me to replicate it, because HE loved it so much!  So... here it is!

Serves 4-6

| | | |
|---|---|---|
| Ears fresh sweet corn, husks removed | 3 | 3 |
| Frozen shelled edamame | 1 lb | 500 g |
| Red bell peppers, chopped | 1-2 | 1-2 |
| Medium red onion, chopped | ½ | ½ |
| Cilantro, finely chopped | 1/4-1/2 cup | 50-125 ml |
| Fresh lime juice | 2 Tbsp | 30 ml |
| Olive oil | 1 Tbsp | 15 ml |
| Garlic clove, pressed or finely minced | 1 | 1 |
| Salt and pepper | | |

Use a sharp knife to remove kernels from the corn, set aside.

Cook edamame according to package directions.  In the last minute or two, add corn kernels. Once cooked, remove from heat, strain, and allow to cool.

Place corn and edamame in a large mixing bowl, along with red peppers, onion, and cilantro. Stir to combine.

In a small mixing bowl or measuring cup, combine lime juice, olive oil, and garlic, whisk to emulsify.  Pour over salad, toss to coat well. Season with salt and pepper to taste.

Cover salad with plastic wrap, chill for at least one hour to allow flavours to combine. Toss one more time, serve cold.

**Variations:**    This is also great with an avocado or two chopped up into it immediately before serving. Also, feel free to with add halved cherry tomatoes, if you so choose.

*Corn, Edamame, and Red Pepper Salad*

# Sweet Corn Bruschetta

This recipe is simple, elegant, and easy to tinker with.  It's beautiful and delicious with the most simple of balsamic vinegars... but is *mind blowingly amazing* if you can get your hands on white peach balsamic vinegar.

Serves 4-6

| | | |
|---|---|---|
| Ears fresh sweet corn, husks removed | 4 | 4 |
| Liquid honey | 1 Tbsp | 15 ml |
| Granulated sugar | 1 Tbsp | 15 ml |
| Balsamic vinegar of choice | 3 Tbsp | 45 ml |
| Fresh basil, cut into thin strips | 1/4 cup | 50 ml |
| Salt | | |
| Pepper | | |
| Baguette | 1 | 1 |
| Olive oil | ~ 1/4 cup | ~ 50 ml |
| Goat Cheese | 6 oz | 170 g |

Using a sharp knife, carefully cut kernels off the ears of corn.    In a large bowl, combine corn kernels, honey, sugar, and balsamic vinegar, tossing to coat. Stir in basil, season with salt and pepper to taste.

Cut baguette into 1/4-1/2" thick slices - I like to cut them at a bit of an angle. Brush both sides of each bread slice with olive oil, arrange on a broiling pan.

Broil bread slices for 3 minutes, flip them all over, and broil for another 2 minutes. Remove from oven, spread each slice with some goat cheese, top with corn mixture. Serve immediately!

**Variations:**

- Add in some diced fresh tomato
- Try chili flakes, for a bit of a kick
- Try different fresh herbs: dill, tarragon, parsley, thyme, mint, cilantro...
- Add a pressed garlic clove
- Swap the goat cheese for mascarpone or cream cheese
- Add a little finely chopped onion

*Sweet Corn Bruschetta*

# Roasted Corn Bread

I love this updated version of traditional corn bread - the roasted flavour from the corn and jalapenos really elevates this cornbread to something special.  For extra roasty flavour, substitute blue cornmeal for regular yellow cornmeal. Serves 12

| | | |
|---|---|---|
| Large jalapenos | 2-3 | 2-3 |
| Ears fresh sweet corn, husks removed | 3 | 3 |
| Olive oil | 1/4 cup | 50 ml |
| Butter | 3/4 cup | 175 ml |
| Granulated sugar | 1 cup | 250 ml |
| Large eggs | 3 | 3 |
| Buttermilk* | 1 ½ cups | 375 ml |
| All-purple flour | 1 ½ cups | 375 ml |
| Yellow cornmeal | 1 ½ cups | 375 ml |
| Baking soda | 1 tsp | 5 ml |
| Salt | 1 tsp | 5 ml |

Preheat oven to 375 F (190 C), grease a 9 x 13" baking pan with pan spray, butter, or shortening.

Cut jalapenos in half, removing ribs and seeds for a more mild bread. Brush peppers and corn cobs with olive oil. Grill corn and peppers until as "done" as you would like - personally, I like some dark grill marks for this, but not an overall char. Remove items as they are ready - the peppers will cook the fastest. Allow everything to cool. Chop up the peppers, use a sharp knife to remove kernels from the corn, set aside.

In a large bowl, cream together butter and  sugar until light and fluffy.  Add in eggs and buttermilk, carefully stir until well incorporated.  In a separate bowl, combine flour, cornmeal, baking soda and salt, stirring until well combined.  Mix the dry ingredients into the wet ingredients, stirring just until combined.  Stir corn and jalapenos into batter, just until distributed. Spread batter into prepared pan. Bake for 35-40 minutes, until a knife or toothpick inserted into the center of the bread comes out clean.

* If you don't have buttermilk, use 1 ½ cups milk mixed with 1 Tbsp lemon juice.

**Variations:**

- Add 1 cup of shredded cheese, if so desired.  Try smoked provolone!
- Add 1+ Tbsp of adobo sauce for an added smokey kick!

*Roasted Corn Bread*

*Spicy Corn Pakoras*

70

# Spicy Corn Pakoras

Pakoras are surprisingly easy to make, and the warmth of the Indian spices pair well with the sweetness of the corn.  As my husband is basically a sentient "dad joke", he likes to refer to these as "paCORNas". The chutney works up very quickly, and is a perfect accompaniment to not only the pakoras, but for roasted corn on the cob!

| | | |
|---|---|---|
| Vegetable oil for deep frying | | |
| Garbanzo flour | 1 1/4 cup | 300 ml |
| White rice flour | 1/4 cup | 50 ml |
| Salt | 2 tsp | 10 ml |
| Curry powder | 2 tsp | 10 ml |
| Cumin | 1 tsp | 5 ml |
| Baking powder | 1/4 tsp | 1 ml |
| Water | 1 cup | 250 ml |
| Ears fresh sweet corn, husks removed | 3 | 3 |
| Finely chopped yam or sweet potato | 1 cup | 250 ml |
| Finely chopped onion | 1 cup | 250 ml |
| Jalapeno peppers finely chopped | 1-2 | 1-2 |
| Cilantro, chopped | ½ cup | 125 ml |

Start heating your vegetable oil to 375 F (190 C) – you'll want at least 2-3" of oil in your pot or deep fryer.

In a large bowl, combine flours, salt, spices, and baking powder. Add water, stir well to form a thick batter. All batter to sit for 5 minutes or so, to soften the bean flour. Use a sharp knife to remove kernels from the corn, mix into batter, along with yam, onion, jalapeno, and cilantro. Stir well, making sure that everything is evenly coated with the batter.

Use an ice cream scoop or two spoons to carefully scoop small amounts (1/4 cup or less) of batter into the preheated oil. Fry for a few minutes on each side, until patties are golden brown. Use a slotted metal spoon to transfer cooked patties to paper towels.  Serve hot, with cilantro-mint chutney.

## Cilantro Mint Chutney

| | | |
|---|---|---|
| Cilantro | 2 bunches | 2 bunches |
| Fresh mint leaves* | 2 bunches | 2 bunches |
| Jalapeno, seeded and chopped | 1 | 1 |
| Large lime, juice of | ½ | ½ |
| Salt | ½ tsp | 2 ml |
| Cumin | 1 tsp | 5 ml |
| Granulated sugar | 1 tsp | 5 ml |

* Mint should be about half the volume of the cilantro

Measure everything but the cilantro into a food processor, pulse into finely chopped – almost a paste.  Add a handful of cilantro, pulse til combined. Add the rest of the cilantro, pulse until well chopped and combined.  Cover and refrigerate until use.

# Sweet Corn Tamales

Tamales using fresh corn in the batter, like this, are a popular breakfast, snack, or dessert food throughout Mexico and Central America, with the names, type of serving, and toppings varying depending on where you are.   You might add cinnamon, eggs, and/or dried fruit, or you might fill it with beef, and/or top it with tomatoes.  Depending on where you are and what mood you're in, you might even get them deep fried!

This version of the recipe is somewhat adapted from tradition, as Masa harina isn't necessarily used throughout Southern America when making these tamales - the fresh corn there is more starchy, and therefore doesn't require the addition of any kind of flour.

Makes 22-28 tamales

Dried corn husks
Ears fresh sweet corn, husks removed     8              8
Masa harina                              3 cups         750 ml
Baking powder                            1 ½ tsp        7 ml
Salt                                     1 ½ tsp        7 ml
Butter or lard                           1 cup          250 ml
Granulated sugar                         2/3 cup        150 ml
Milk, optional
Crema or sour cream, optional
Queso fresco, optional
Lime wedges, optional

Soak corn husks in hot water for 30 minutes.

Use a sharp knife to cut kernels from corn, place in food processor, blitz till smooth

In a large bowl, mix masa harina, baking powder, and salt. Set aside.

Cream together butter and sugar until fluffy.  Add to masa harina mixture, mix well before adding corn puree.  Allow dough to rest for 30 minutes.

If the dough is too thick to be spreadable (should be about the consistency of peanut butter), add a little milk to thin it out a bit.

Now, time to wrap the tamales. From everything I read, there's about 10 million ways you can do this. As most involved an open side – something I was NOT interested in – here's how I do it, using about 1/3 cup of batter to each tamal:

I went traditional and used long strips of (broken or otherwise useless) corn husks to tie this off. Feel free to do that if you'd like - but using kitchen twine is quicker and easier, if you have some on hand.

Depending on how the wrap went, some tamales may require 2 ties. It's all good.

Repeat process until all of the batter is used up.

Place tamales in a large steamer. Depending on your equipment, you may need to do this in several batches. We used a turkey fryer over propane burner! (Which is actually our home brewing setup!)

Put enough water in the bottom to almost touch the bottom of the steam basket (but not quite!), and steam for about 1 hours, until dough is cooked through and firmed up.

Serve hot, drizzled with crema or sour cream, sprinkled with queso fresco, and a squeeze of lime!

Also: These can be frozen. We froze them IN the corn husk wrappers, stored in freezer bags. We bring a bag out as we need it, allow to thaw, and then reheat, with or without removing the husk first.

**Variations:**

- For some or all of the tamales, spread the batter into seeded halves of poblano peppers before wrapping and steaming.

- For some or all of the tamales, bury a stick of cheese in the batter before wrapping and steaming

- Try mixing a small can or two of mild chopped chilies into the batter. This is especially good when filling the tamales with cheese, in my opinion!

*Sweet Corn Tamales*

*Hearty Corn and Black Bean Soup*

# Main Dishes

## Hearty Corn and Black Bean Soup

When the weather starts to turn, and the first few cold nights appear... this is a great way to welcome fall. Thick, warm, rich, and satisfying!  If you would like to omit the beer, feel free to substitute with more chicken stock

Serves 6-8

| Large onions, chopped | 2 | 2 |
|---|---|---|
| Bacon, chopped | 1 lb | 500 g |
| Dry black beans | 2 lbs | 1000 g |
| Chicken stock | 12 ½ cups | 3 L |
| Light tasting beer, such as Corona | 12-24 oz | 1 ½ - 3 cups |
| Ears fresh sweet corn, husks removed | 6 | 6 |
| Limes, juice and zest of | 2 | 2 |
| Celery ribs, chopped | 6 | 6 |
| Green bell peppers, chopped | 3 | 3 |
| Red bell peppers, chopped | 2 | 2 |
| Yellow bell pepper, chopped | 1 | 1 |
| Jalapeno peppers, finely chopped | 3 | 3 |
| Garlic cloves, pressed or minced | 6 | 6 |
| Ground cumin | 2 tsp | 20 ml |
| Salt | 1 tsp | 5 ml |
| Pepper | 1 tsp | 5 ml |

In a large, heavy pot, saute onions and bacon until bacon is cooked but not crispy. Add black beans, chicken stock, and beer, bring to a boil. Once mixture comes to a boil, stir it once, cover it with a lid, and remove from heat. Allow to sit for 1 hour.

Once an hour has passed, bring pot to a boil once more.  Reduce heat, simmer for one hour, stirring frequently.

Using a sharp knife, carefully cut kernels off the ears of corn, add to a pot along with lime juice/zest, celery, peppers, garlic, and seasonings. Continue to simmer for another 20 minutes, or until beans and all vegetables are tender, and soup is THICK. Serve hot, topped with cheddar cheese, sour cream, and /or crumbled bacon.

# Roasted Corn Chowder

This is a great base recipe for chowder, and can be customized in many ways. It's a little bit of effort, but very much worth it!  For a little more depth of flavour, you can use chicken or vegetable broth in place of the water, if desired!

| | | |
|---|---|---|
| Ears fresh sweet corn, husks removed | 6-7 | 6-7 |
| Olive oil | 2 Tbsp | 30 ml |
| Red potatoes | 4-5 | 4-5 |
| Water | 2 cups | 500 ml |
| Celery ribs | 2 | 2 |
| Small onion | 1 | 1 |
| Olive oil | 1 Tbsp | 15 ml |
| Heavy cream | 1 ½ cups | 375 ml |
| Salt and pepper | | |

Brush 3-4 corn cobs with olive oil, grill corn until as "done" as you would like - personally, I like some dark grill marks for this, but not an overall char. Set aside, allowing them to cool.

Using a sharp knife, carefully cut kernels off remaining ears of corn, add to a blender or food processor with 1 cup of the water. Puree until very smooth, around 2 minutes.

Wash potatoes, peel if desired.  Chop potatoes into ½" chunks, set aside

In a medium sized pot, saute celery and onions with olive oil, until veggies are translucent and tender.  Add corn puree, remaining cup of water, and potatoes. Bring to a boil, reduce heat, and simmer until potatoes are tender.

Carefully cut kernels off roasted cobs of corn, puree with ½ cup of heavy cream until somewhat smooth, about 30 seconds.  Add roast corn puree and remaining heavy cream to the pot, simmer until heated through.  Season with salt and pepper to taste.

**Variations:**

- Add some roasted red peppers along with the roasted corn puree
- Add some fresh basil and Parmesan cheese
- Add a couple of roasted jalapenos, finely chopped
- Add some crumbled bacon
- For a cheesy corn soup, add 1-2 cups shredded cheese along with the roasted corn puree, to taste.

*Roasted Corn Chowder*

# Cod and Corn Chowder

Sometimes, you want a chowder that comes together quickly and easily - and this one will not disappoint!  The mushrooms, red pepper, corn, and cod not only taste really good together, they produce a chowder that's actually fairly pretty - a departure from the usual bland whiteness of fish chowders.   Makes about 6 servings

| | | |
|---|---|---|
| Bacon, sliced into small pieces | ½ lb | 250 g |
| Small onion, finely chopped | ½ | ½ |
| Crimini/bella mushrooms, sliced | 4-6 oz | 125-170 g |
| Red pepper, finely chopped | 1 | 1 |
| Medium-large red potatoes | 4 | 4 |
| Water or chicken or vegetable broth | 3 ½ cups | 875 ml |
| Ears fresh sweet corn, husks removed | 3 | 3 |
| Milk | 1 ½ cups | 375 ml |
| Heavy cream | 2 cups | 500 ml |
| Cod loins, cubed | 3-4 lbs | 1500 g - 2 kg |
| Salt and pepper | | |

In a large saucepan, cook bacon over medium heat until cooked but not yet crispy. Add onion, mushrooms, and red pepper. Continue to cook, stirring every once in awhile, until onions are translucent and all veggies are softened.

Wash potatoes, cut into ½" chunks. Add to pot, along with the water or broth. Bring heat to high, cook at a rolling boil for 10-15 minutes or until potatoes are almost cooked through.

As the potatoes are cooking, use a sharp knife to carefully cut kernels off the ears of corn. Reserve half of the kernels, add remaining kernels to a food processor or blender, along with milk. Process till smooth.

When potatoes are about ready, add corn puree and heavy cream, bring back to a boil. Add cod and reserved corn kernels, continue to cook for another 7 minutes or so, until cod is cooked through. Season with salt and pepper to taste, serve hot.

**Variations:**

This is a great base recipe that not only tastes fabulous as-is, it also takes well to all kinds of seasoning added, should you desire.  Try adding a small handful of dried summer savoury, or some chopped fresh tarragon, basil, or dill at the very end of cooking.  Alternatively, smoked serrano powder packs a powerful flavour punch. Used VERY judiciously, a small amount goes very well in this chowder!

*Cod and Corn Chowder*

# "Midwest Goes Southwest" Hotdish

Back when I first moved to Minnesota, I was a little horrified when someone explained the concept of "hotdish" casserole to me.  It just sounded so ... bland.

If hotdish was something I'd need to do, I needed to come up with something far more flavourful than cream of mushroom soup. This is what resulted.

| | | |
|---|---|---|
| Boneless skinless chicken breast | 1 ½ lb | 750 g |
| Olive oil | 2 Tbsp | 30 ml |
| Medium onion, thinly sliced | 1 | 1 |
| Jalapeno pepper, finely chopped | 1 | 1 |
| Poblano peppers, thinly sliced | 2 | 2 |
| Garlic cloves, chopped | 4 | 4 |
| Ears fresh sweet corn, husks removed | 3 | 3 |
| Cans black beans (15 oz each) | 2 | 2 |
| Red pepper flakes | ½ tsp | 2 ml |
| Cumin powder | 1 ½ tsp | 7 ml |
| Cans condensed cheese soup | 2 | 2 |
| Salsa of choice | ½ cup | 125 ml |
| Sliced black olives | ½ cup | 125 ml |
| Shredded Monterey jack cheese | 2 cups | 500 ml |
| Frozen tater tots | 2 lb | 1 Kg |

Preheat oven to 350 F (180 C)

Slice chicken breast into bite sized pieces. Add to a large pan, along with olive oil. Cook over medium heat until chicken is browned, but not necessarily cooked all the way through.

Add onion, peppers, and garlic to the pan, saute until peppers are tender.

Using a sharp knife, carefully cut kernels off the ears of corn, add to the pan along. Strain and rinse black beans, add to the pan along with red pepper flakes and cumin. Stir well, cook for 2 minutes.

Pour mixture into a 9 x 13 casserole dish or baking pan. Stir in condensed soup, salsa, and black olives, mix well to coat everything evenly.

Sprinkle shredded cheese over mixture. Arrange tater tots in a single layer on top of the cheese. Bake at 350 for 50 minutes. Serve hot!

*"Midwest Goes Southwest" Hotdish*

# Cottage Pie

Cottage pie is a variation on the traditional shepherd's pie dish, which uses lamb. This recipe makes a lot of food—two baking pans' worth. Cool and freeze one for future meals and use the other for immediate eating. Serves 12+

| | | |
|---|---|---|
| Red or gold potatoes | 5 lbs | 2 Kg |
| Lean ground beef | 2 lb | 1 Kg |
| Carrots, peeled and grated | 2 | 2 |
| Parsnips, peeled and grated | 2 | 2 |
| Medium onion, peeled and grated | 1 | 1 |
| Garlic cloves, pressed or minced | 2 | 2 |
| Beef broth, divided | 1 3/4 cups | 425 ml |
| Cornstarch | 2 Tbsp | 30 ml |
| Pepper, divided | 2 tsp | 10 ml |
| Salt, divided | 2 tsp | 10 ml |
| Dried summer savoury | ½ tsp | 2 ml |
| Chopped fresh parsley | 1/4 cup | 50 ml |
| Ears fresh sweet corn, husks removed | 8 | 8 |
| Heavy cream | 1 ½ cups | 375 ml |
| Butter | 1/4 cup | 50 ml |
| Sour cream | 1 ½ cups | 375 ml |

Peel potatoes if desired, chop into 2 inch chunks. In a large pot of boiling water, cook potatoes until tender. While potatoes are cooking, combine ground beef, grated vegetables, and garlic in a large skillet. Cook over medium-high heat, stirring frequently, until meat is cooked through and veggies are tender, about 5 minutes. Whisk together 1½ cups beef broth and cornstarch until smooth. Pour over meat mixture, and season with 1 teaspoon pepper, ½ teaspoon salt, savoury, and parsley. Continue to cook, stirring to combine, until broth mixture starts to thicken. Remove from heat.

Use a sharp knife to remove kernels from the corn. Place kernels in a medium pot along with heavy cream. Bring to a boil, reduce heat, and simmer for 10 minutes. Remove from heat, and season with salt to taste.

When potatoes are tender, drain and transfer to a large mixing bowl or the bowl of a stand mixer. Mash or whip for 30 seconds or so, until potatoes have broken down a bit. Add butter, remaining ¼ cup broth, and sour cream, and continue to beat until smooth. Stir in remaining 1½ teaspoons salt and 1 tsp pepper.

Preheat broiler to high. Divide meat mixture evenly between two 9x13–inch pans. Divide corn mixture between the two pans, spreading evenly over the meat mixture. Spread potato mixture evenly over the corn, and broil until potatoes are as browned as you like them.  Serve hot, or chill and freeze up to 2 months for future use.

*Cottage Pie*

# Chicken & Corn Pot Pie

Comfort food at its finest!  On a chilly fall day, what could be better than your own personal little pot of warm, gooey pot pie, topped with a flaky, crisp puff pastry cap?  Yum!        Makes 4 large servings

| | | |
|---|---|---|
| Rotisserie chicken | 1 | 1 |
| Ears fresh sweet corn, husks removed | 6 | 6 |
| Chicken broth | 5 cups | 1 1/4 L |
| Unsalted butter | 3/4 cup | 175 ml |
| Large onion, chopped | 1 | 1 |
| Ribs celery, chopped | 4 | 4 |
| All purpose flour | 3/4 cup | 175 ml |
| Heavy cream | 1/4 cup | 50 ml |
| Fresh parsley, finely chopped | 1/3 cup | 75 ml |
| Salt and pepper | | |
| Frozen puff pastry sheets, thawed | 2 | 2 |
| Large egg | 1 | 1 |

Preheat the oven to 350 F (180 C).  Remove meat from the chicken, cut into bite sized pieces. Set aside. Use a sharp knife to remove kernels from the corn. Reserve corn kernels with the chicken pieces, add cobs to a medium pot along with chicken broth. Bring to a boil, reduce heat, and simmer for 10 minutes.  Discard cobs, set broth aside.

In a large pot, melt butter over medium heat. Add onion and celery, cook - stirring frequently - until vegetables are tender and translucent. Reduce heat to low, add flour, and stir well to incorporate. Cook for 1 more minute, stirring constantly. Add heavy cream, stirring well until smooth and thickened. Add chicken, corn, and chicken broth, bring just to a boil.  Remove from heat, stir in the fresh parsley, season with salt and pepper to taste. Divide the filling among 4 large individual ramekins.

Cut each thawed puff pastry sheet in half, lay one piece across the top of each filled ramekin. (Feel free to press the edges down around the ramekin rim, I don't bother!) Whisk egg with 2 Tbsp of water, use a pastry brush to brush the top of each pot pie cap.  Arrange ramekins on a cookie sheet, bake for about 25 minutes, until tops are puffy and golden brown.

**Variations:**

- Add 6 strips crumbled crispy bacon into the filling.- Puree half the reserved corn kernels with a bit of the broth, add puree back to the broth, stir well.

*Chicken & Corn Pot Pie*

# Savoury Corn Cheesecake

Who says cheesecake is only for dessert?  This savoury version is best served at least slightly warm... I like it best chilled first, and reheated to HOT in the microwave. Yum!

| | | |
|---|---|---|
| Almond meal/ flour | 1 1/4 cups | 300 ml |
| Grated Parmesan cheese | ½ cup | 125 ml |
| Butter, melted | 1/3 cup | 75 ml |
| Pepper | Pinch | Pinch |

Combine all ingredients until completely incorporated and moistened. Evenly distribute across the bottom of a 9" spring form pan. Press ingredients firmly, extending crust partway up the sides of the pan.  Chill for at least 1 hour.

| | | |
|---|---|---|
| Ears fresh sweet corn, husks removed | 3 | 3 |
| Milk | ½ cup | 125 ml |
| Small onion, diced | ½ | ½ |
| Garlic cloves, pressed or minced | 2 | 2 |
| Cream cheese, softened | 1 ½ lbs | 750 g |
| Shredded Provolone cheese | 1 cup | 250 ml |
| Sour cream | ½ cup | 125 ml |
| Large eggs | 6 | 6 |
| Heavy cream | 1 cup | 250 ml |
| Salt | 1 tsp | 5 ml |
| Pepper | 1/4- ½ tsp | 1-2 ml |

Preheat oven to 425 F (220 C).  Using a sharp knife, carefully cut kernels off the ears of corn, add to a food processor or blender, along with milk, onion, and garlic. Puree until very smooth, about 2 minutes.  Transfer to a large mixing bowl.

In food processor, combine cream cheese, provolone, sour cream, and eggs. Carefully stream in heavy cream, process just until well combined and smooth. Pour cheese mixture into corn mixture, stir til well combined. Season with salt and pepper. Gently pour batter into prepared crust, bake for 15 minutes. After 15 minutes, turn the oven down to 325 F (160 C) and bake for 50 minutes. Once baking time is complete, turn off the oven and allow cheesecake cake to cool – WITHOUT opening the door! – for 2 hours.

Note: While this cheesecake is fantastic as it is, it also works well when topped with any number of complementary items.  Try roasted corn kernels, roasted red pepper, pesto, or crumbled bacon!

*Savoury Corn Cheesecake*

# Sweet Corn Risotto

Risotto is one of those dishes that many assume to be difficult to make, when that couldn't be further from the truth. In addition to being easy to make, I find the repetition of the "add liquid, stir" steps to be relaxing!

Note: A dry white wine works best with this. Don't use cooking wine, though... for anything, really! It's salty and doesn't taste right - the point is to add <u>good</u> flavour to the dish!

While the alcohol cooks off while making this dish, you can definitely substitute more broth for the  wine, if you'd like to omit it.

| | | |
|---|---|---|
| Ears fresh sweet corn, husks removed | 3 | 3 |
| Chicken stock or broth | 6 cups | 1 ½ L |
| Dry white wine of choice | 2/3 cup | 150 ml |
| Olive oil | 1 Tbsp | 15 ml |
| Medium onion, finely chopped | 1 | 1 |
| Garlic cloves, pressed or finely minced | 2 | 2 |
| Arborio rice | 1 ½ cups | 375 ml |
| Fresh tarragon, finely chopped | 1-2 Tbsp | 15-30 ml |
| Butter | 2 Tbsp | 30 ml |
| Parmesan cheese | 1 cup | 250 ml |
| Salt and pepper | | |

Use a sharp knife to remove kernels from the corn. Reserve corn kernels in a bowl, add cobs to a large pot, along with chicken broth and white wine.  Bring to a boil, reduce heat, and simmer for 10 minutes.  Discard cobs, turn heat down to low.

In a large saucepan, combine olive oil, and onion.  Cook over medium heat, stirring frequently, until onion is soft and translucent. Add garlic, rice, and about ½ cup of the chicken broth. Cook, stirring frequently, until almost all of the liquid is absorbed by the rice.  One cup at a time, repeat this until you have about 1 cup of liquid left.

Along with final amount of liquid, add fresh corn kernels and tarragon. Once rice is fully cooked and risotto is creamy and perfect, add butter and Parmesan cheese. Stir until everything is well combined and melty, season with salt and pepper to taste. Serve hot.

Variation:  I love this with seafood on top - a bit of warm cooked crab, lobster, or scallops. Yum!

*Sweet Corn Risotto*

# Ham & Corn Skewers with Pineapple Bourbon Glaze

This recipe is based on my Easter ham recipe... far too good to relegate to a single season.

The flavours that work so well with that ham - pineapple juice, honey, mustard, and bourbon - not only work well with a whole roasted ham, but with corn on the cob, also! A great marriage of flavours, with far less effort than putting on a whole Easter spread!

Serves 4-6

| | | |
|---|---|---|
| Fully cooked ham | 3 lbs | 1 ½ Kg |
| Ears fresh sweet corn, husks removed | 2-3 | 2-3 |
| Onion, sliced | 1 | 1 |
| Green peppers, cut into 1" squares | 2 | 2 |
| Large can pineapple chunks, optional | 1 | 1 |
| Pineapple juice | ½ cup | 125 ml |
| Bourbon | 1/4 cup | 50 ml |
| Liquid honey | 1/4 cup | 50 ml |
| Dijon mustard | 1 Tbsp | 15 ml |
| Garlic cloves, pressed or minced | 2 | 2 |
| Salt and pepper | | |

Trim ham as necessary, and cut into 1" cubes, place into a large mixing bowl.

Use a sharp knife to cut corn cobs into 1.5" thick rounds. Add cut corn to the mixing bowl, along with , green peppers, and pineapple chunks, if using.

In a smaller mixing bowl, whisk together all remaining ingredients, seasoning with salt and pepper to taste. Pour over skewer ingredients, toss to coat everything. Cover with plastic wrap, chill in the fridge for 1+ hours (up to a day).

Heat the grill and thread skewer ingredients onto metal grill skewers.

Grill skewers until done, brushing occasionally with remaining marinade – the time will vary depending on your grill.

Serve hot.

*Ham and Corn Skewers with Pineapple Bourbon Glaze*

# Grilled Corn Quesadillas

Quesadillas have been a favorite of mine since I was a kid. Best of all was one that utilized the fairly standard ingredients with the addition of corn.  Nowadays, I prefer my quesadillas with many of those ingredients grilled beforehand, lending a wonderful, smoky taste to a traditional favorite.  Serves 4

| | | |
|---|---|---|
| Red bell pepper | 1 | 1 |
| Poblano pepper | 1 | 1 |
| Medium onion, peeled | 1 | 1 |
| Jalapeno peppers | 1-2 | 1-2 |
| Ears fresh sweet corn, husks removed | 3 | 3 |
| Olive oil | 1/4 cup | 50 ml |
| Chopped cilantro | 1/4 cup | 50 ml |
| Cumin, optional | 1/4-1/2 tsp | 1-2 ml |
| Salt and pepper | | |
| Large flour tortillas | 4 | 4 |
| Shredded Monterey Jack cheese | 12 oz | 375 g |
| Salsa | | |
| Sour cream | | |

Preheat grill, coat with nonstick grill spray. Slice red and poblano peppers into large flat pieces and onion into ½-inch-thick slices. Cut jalapenos in half, removing ribs and seeds if you prefer a milder quesadilla. Brush peppers, onion, and corn cobs with olive oil. Grill everything until as "done" as you like (I prefer some dark grill marks but not an overall char). Remove items as they are ready; the peppers will cook the fastest. Allow everything to cool.

Chop peppers and onion; place in a bowl. Use a sharp knife to remove kernels from the corn, and add to the bowl along with cilantro and cumin if using. Stir well, and season with salt and pepper to taste.

Arrange 4 tortillas on work surface. Divide half of the cheese among the tortillas, spreading across half of each round. Divide corn mixture among the tortillas, spreading evenly over the cheese, to within 1 inch of the edges. Top evenly with remaining cheese.  For each quesadilla, fold unadorned half of tortilla over the filling, press gently.

Brush quesadillas with olive oil (or spray), and grill for a few minutes, until cheese is melty. Carefully flip each quesadilla to grill on the other side for a minute or two. Cut into wedges and serve hot, with salsa and sour cream.

*Grilled Corn Quesadillas*

*Low Country Boil*

# Low Country Boil (AKA "Frogmore Stew")

This Southern dish can be done so many ways, and I never do two exactly the same. It can be a quick and easy meal for 2, or it can be the basis for a GREAT cookout party with friends. Additionally, it can be a frugal, thrifty thing... or as extravagant as you want.

The main ingredients are very basic: Corn, Smoked Sausage, Potatoes, Shrimp, Lemons, Seasoning. You get a big pot of seasoned water boiling, and one by one add the ingredients to the pot, starting with potatoes (take the longest to cook), and ending with shrimp (take very little time to cook).

Of course, I never do anything the way you're supposed to.. and besides, I'm not even southern. That means I'm exempt from any rules that may be applied here, right? The big change I like to make is with the seasoning. You're "supposed to" use Old Bay Seasoning for this. Not only is that boring, but the salt content is obscene, and besides.. customization is always more fun! I like using a mix of fresh (onions, garlic, green onions, jalapenos, etc) and dried (sage, pepper, dried mustard, parsley, bay leaves, etc) ingredients to flavour my broth.

You can also start your broth off in different ways – use some chicken broth, boil fresh shrimp shells (without the shrimp in them!) for added flavour – just remove the shells before adding your food and other seasonings in! Also, adding a can or two of beer to your water / broth adds a great flavour. Any of these is a much better option than just water and Old Bay Seasoning, in my not so humble opinion!

The ingredients are also customizable. Corn, Potatoes, Shrimp, and Sausage are a good solid foundation.. but feel free to add clams, mussels, and even crab legs. It's your meal!

Now that I've made the whole thing sound way more complicated than it is, let me give you a basic recipe for it, and let you just have at it! This makes a substantial amount of food, so don't be surprised if you have leftovers. It also makes ridiculously good food, so don't be surprised if you don't have leftovers because everyone gorged till they had nothing left to eat!

Broth:

1 onion for every 3 people being served – quartered
1 lemon for every 3 or so people being served, quartered
Beer – Optional, but about 1 can for every 2-3 people being served, if using.
Chicken broth (optional, use as much or as little as you want)
Garlic – as much as you want

Green onions (optional.. a couple chopped for every few people is usually good)
Jalapenos, habaneros, or whatever (optional, chop a few for every few people)
Dried sage – 1 tsp for every 3 or so being served
Pepper – as much as you like
Dried mustard powder – as much as you'd like.
Bay Leaves – 1 for every few being served
Dried Parsley – add a handful for colour.

Main Ingredients (Approximate amounts per person):

| | | |
|---|---|---|
| New red potatoes, halved or quartered | 1/3 lb | 140 g |
| Smoked sausage (like Kielbassa) | ½ lb | 250 g |
| Raw shrimp, thawed if frozen | 1/3 lb | 140 g |
| Ears fresh sweet corn, husks removed | 1-2 | 1-2 |
| Whatever else you want – clams, crab, mussels, etc | | |

Get a pot of an appropriate size for the amount of food you're looking to cook. The more people being served, the bigger the pot!

Add chicken stock and/or beer if you're going to, as well as everything else from the broth ingredients that you're using. Also, whatever else you want to use to flavour it. Add water, filling the pot about 1/3 full (to start). Bring it to a boil.

Add potatoes and sausage, adding more water if necessary. Sausage doesn't take long to cook, but it will add a great flavour to the water – and potatoes. Cook for 30 minutes or so.

Add the corn, cook another 5 minutes.

Add the shrimp, and any other seafood you may want to add. Cook another 5 minutes, or until it's done – shrimp should be pink, clams and mussels fully open, etc. Discard any mussels, clams, etc that do not open.

Traditionally, you're supposed to strain everything out, and dump it out in the middle of a newspaper-covered table for a savage free for all. While this is great fun for a cookout, we usually end up straining everything into a large mixing bowl.

In either case, serve it up with cocktail sauce, Dijon mustard, or whatever else you'd like to dip your food in. Dig in!

Pro tip:  Leftover potatoes from a well seasoned low country boil make the BEST hashbrowns!

*Quick Corn, Tomato, and Basil Chutney*

# Condiments & Beverages

## Quick Corn, Tomato, and Basil Chutney

This thick, non-pickled relish is a great way to add a ton of flavour to basic meat dishes,  Try over a pan fried pork chop - or pork loin roast! -  roasted chicken, or even with crab cakes!

Makes about 2 cups

| | | |
|---|---|---|
| Ears fresh sweet corn, husks removed | 2 | 2 |
| Cherry tomatoes, quartered | 2 cups | 500 ml |
| Fresh basil leaves | 1/3 cup | 75 ml |
| Thinly sliced green onions | 1/4 cup | 50 ml |
| Red wine vinegar | 2 Tbsp | 30 ml |
| Olive oil | 1 Tbsp | 15 ml |
| Salt and pepper | | |

Using a sharp knife, carefully cut kernels off the ears of corn.  Please corn kernels in a nonstick frying pan, along with quartered cherry tomatoes.  Saute over high heat for about 5 minutes.

Remove from heat.  Slice basil leaves into thin ribbons ("chiffonade"), stir basil and green onions into corn mixture, allow to cool to room temperature.

Whisk together red wine vinegar and olive oil until emulsified.  Toss with cooled corn and tomato mixture, season with salt and pepper to taste.

Serve chilled or reheated.

Variation:  If you want to get more elaborate - and enjoy a taste payoff! - try grilling or roasting the tomatoes and corn before mixing ingredients together.

# Sweet Corn Relish

When originally developing this recipe for " Sweet Corn Spectacular", I left a big jar of this corn relish at a friend's house, as a "welcome home" gift - we'd been checking up on her cats when she was gone.  It didn't take long for her to message me to thank me, saying that "Holy crap, it's DELICIOUS". When I let her know that we had plenty, if she ever wanted more... she surprised me with her followup:

"I will take as much of this corn business as you're willing to give me. I want to pour it in a kiddie pool and lounge around in it :p"

I... think she liked it.  You may want to make even more of this, than the 5 quarts or so that this makes!

| | | |
|---|---|---|
| Ears fresh corn, husks removed | 24 | 24 |
| Large green bell peppers | 4 | 4 |
| Large onions | 2 | 2 |
| Large tomatoes | 2-3 | 2-3 |
| Celery ribs | 4-5 | 4-5 |
| Jalapeno peppers | 2 | 2 |
| Granulated sugar | 1½ cups | 375 ml |
| Salt | 1/4 cup | 50 ml |
| Turmeric | 2 tsp | 10 ml |
| Celery seed | 1 Tbsp | 15 ml |
| Mustard powder | 2 tsp | 10 ml |
| White vinegar | 5 cups | 1250 ml |

Use a sharp knife to remove the kernels from the ears of corn, place kernels into a large pot.  Chop bell peppers, onions, tomatoes, celery, and jalapenos (removing ribs and seeds if you'd like a less spicy relish), add them to the pot.

In a large bowl, mix together sugar, salt, turmeric, celery seed, and mustard powder. Add this mixture to the pot, stir well, then add the vinegar.  Heat to a boil, reduce heat and simmer for about 40 minutes.

Ladle into hot, sterilized canning jars. Affix sterilized lids and rims, process in a hot water bath for 15 minutes.  (Add 5 minutes for altitudes above 1000 ft, add 10 minutes for altitudes over 6000 ft).

Allow to cool overnight.  Check all lids for a proper seal - it should have sucked down into  vacuum seal, as it cooled.  Store properly sealed jars for later use, refrigerate any that did not seal, for use in the coming weeks.

*Sweet Corn Relish*

*Pickled Corn on the Cob*

# Pickled Corn on the Cob

Did you know that you can pickle just about any kind of vegetable you can imagine?  As I discovered on my "Great Pickling Binge of 2012", slices of whole corn on the cob pickle beautifully!  Personally, I like to add several big slices of jalapeno pepper to each jar - They're pretty AND add a ton of flavour!

A few notes about pickling:

1. The amount of brine you're going to need will vary widely depend on the shape and size of your corn cob slices, the size of jar you use, and how well you pack them into the jar. Have a lot of extra vinegar on hand, and either make more brine than you think you'll need, or be prepared to make more as you go. As a general idea of scale, the recipe below made about 6 quart jars of pickles, packed VERY tightly. Your mileage will likely vary!

2. Pickling salt is usually available with the canning supplies in any grocery store. You'll want to use this, rather than regular table salt – the anti-caking additives in table salt can make your pickle brine go murky and ugly.

3. While you can use previously-used jars for canning (when WELL washed and sterilized!), you need new lids for each new batch. Safety first!

Pickles:

| | | |
|---|---|---|
| Ears fresh sweet corn, husks removed | 12 | 12 |

Brine:

| | | |
|---|---|---|
| White vinegar | 8 cups | 2 L |
| Water | 8 cups | 2 L |
| Pickling salt | 1 cup | 250 ml |

Per pint jar (2x for quart jars):

| | | |
|---|---|---|
| Dill seed | ½ - 1 tsp | 2-5 ml |
| Garlic cloves, peeled and cut in half | 1-2 | 1-2 |
| Black peppercorns | 1/4 tsp | 1 ml |
| Mustard seed | 1/4 tsp | 1 ml |
| Jalapeno slices (optional) | | |

Canning Equipment:

Clean, sterilized canning jars & rings
New, never-used, sterilized canning lids
Canning funnel
LARGE pot to process them in
Jar lifter (nice to have, not necessary if you can handle pain!)

Use a very sharp, heavy knife to cut cobs of corn into 1 ½" wide disks.

Fill your LARGE pot with at least 6" of water, put on medium or high heat to bring it to a boil as you prepare your brine.

In another pot (NOT the canning pot!), combine vinegar, water, and salt. Bring to a boil, stirring well to dissolve the salt. As the brine heats up, measure your "per jar" ingredients into your sterilized jars. Arrange your sliced corn cobs into the jars, packing them tightly – seriously, try to cram as many pieces into each jar as you can!

Once brine comes to a boil, use a canning funnel to pour brine into prepared jars, leaving about ½" head space. Wipe off the top edges of the jar with a clean, wet towel, top each with a new, sterilized lid, and carefully screw on a clean lid ring. I like to use a kitchen towel for this, the jars are HOT! Carefully place your jars of pickles into the boiling water pot, allow to process for 25 minutes. CAREFULLY remove them, allow to cool overnight.

The next morning, check to make sure that all of the jars achieved a proper seal – try to push down in the middle of each lid. If it "pops", it did not seal. Any jars that didn't seal should be put in the fridge and used in the next few weeks.

Leave the jars alone for at least a few days, to allow the flavours to permeate the pickles. Store in a cool, dark area (ideally) for up to 1 year, chill well before eating.

# Compound Butters

Compound butter is an extremely simple thing – you take a soft stick of butter, and mix STUFF into it. Spices, fresh herbs, zest, finely chopped vegetables… whatever. Literally – WHATEVER… if you can think of some sort of flavourful aromatic, odds are you can make a compound butter with it. This isn't so much a recipe, as it is a springboard for your own ideas and recipes.

The casual nature of that description doesn't really do justice to compound butter's place in cuisine – it's a very basic part of fine French cooking. Compound butters were made ahead of time to add flavour to almost any dish. Melted compound butter would serve as a substitute for a sauce, while room temperature butters would be served alongside steak, vegetables, seafood. Anchovy butter was (is?) quite popular, along with flavours such as truffle, tarragon, garlic… even wine.

Beyond historical use, compound butters are great in any modern kitchen - Melt them over steak, use them as a sauce, melt over popcorn, spread on a sandwich. Given that compound butters can be made either sweet or savoury, the possibilities are endless.  For the purposes of this cookbook, however... compound butters are amazing on corn on the cob.

For compound butters intended for use on corn, specifically, you can really run wild on the flavours you choose, as the corn provides a really flexible base flavour. Basically, any fresh/dried herb or spice is fair game, as well as other items: bacon, dried mushrooms, anchovies, mustard, pesto, crushed peppercorns, etc.

Some other ideas:

- Dijon mustard compound butter is particularly amazing on roasted corn on the cob.
- Caramelized onion.
- Finely chopped canned chipotle peppers, along with some of the adobo sauce they came in.
- Curry powder and a little chopped cilantro & fresh mint  add a bit of Asian flair to your corn.
- For an Italian flavour, use grated Parmesan cheese, oregano, basil and a little garlic powder
- Go Southwest with some chili powder and cumin.
- Finely chopped jalapenos.

Other savoury flavours that work well with corn, alone or in combination:  chervil, chives, cumin, lemon balm, lemon-garlic, lime and chili,  onion, paprika, parsley, saffron, sage, thyme.

While savoury flavours are most popular for corn on the cob, don't overlook the sweet possibilities. Adding a tablespoon or so of sugar or honey along with sweeter ingredients can really yield a spectacular taste on corn. Any kind of citrus zest works well, and - believe it or not - powdered cinnamon is a popular choice in some areas.

How do you make it? Simple!

Take a stick or two of butter, allow it to come to room temperature – you'll want it nice and soft.

Stir in whatever flavouring agents you like, mixing and matching as desired. I like to go 2-3 Tbsp of solids (fresh herbs, zest, whatever) or around ~1- 1.5 Tbsp of powders per stick of butter, as a rough guide… but there's a lot of room to play. Make sure to pack a lot of flavour into it (½ tsp of, say, curry powder will NOT cut it!) I try to vary colours to make it look pretty – for instance, mint & cilantro with curry powder!

Whip it until everything is well distributed. Refrigerate for about 10 minutes, or just long enough for it to firm up slightly – but still be workable. Dump it out onto a section of plastic wrap and roll it into a log. (Alternatively, mush it into an appropriately sized ramekin or other vessel.) Chill until firmly set.

Try to use the butter within one week, if stored in the fridge. If you'd like to hang on to it for longer than that, it can be stored in the freezer for about a month.

Oh, and be sure to consider sharing the love – logs or little ceramic pots of compound butter make great hostess gifts!

Logs: Peel the plastic wrap off your well chilled – FIRM – log of compound butter. Wrap tightly with a clean pieces of plastic wrap, before rolling it up in a piece of something more decorative – parchment paper, cellophane, craft paper, etc. Tie off either end with some twine or ribbon, and label it with a flavour if you want.

Pots: press your still-soft compound butter into a ceramic ramekin, right after mixing it up. Use the back side of a spoon to create a pretty swirl on top of the butter, chill till firm. Place chilled ramekin in the middle of a large piece of cellophane, draw all of the sides and corners up, and secure on top of the ramekin with a bow – ribbon or twine.

*Compound Butters*

# Corn Cob Jelly

This jelly is a great way to use up the cobs left over from various "cut the kernels off the cob" recipes. When it's finished, it actually tastes a lot like honey!

Makes about 3 pints

| | | |
|---|---|---|
| Corn cobs | 12 | 12 |
| Water | 8 cups | 2 L |
| Fresh lemon juice | 1 Tbsp | 15 ml |
| Powdered fruit pectin | 1 box | 1 box |
| Granulated sugar | 4 cups | 1000 ml |
| Yellow food colouring, optional | | |

If your cobs aren't "leftover", cut the kernels off and save for another recipe.

Add corn cobs and water to a large pot, bring to a full rolling boil for 10-20 minutes, or until liquid is reduced to about half the original volume.

Strain liquid through a couple layers of cheesecloth, measure. Add a little water, if needed, to bring the amount up to 3 cups. Return liquid to pot, add lemon juice and pectin, bring to a boil. Add sugar to pot, stir well to dissolve.

Bring pot to a full rolling boil for one complete minute, remove from heat, Add a little food colouring, if desired.

Ladle into hot, sterilized canning jars. Affix sterilized lids and rims, process in a hot water bath for 15 minutes. (Add 5 minutes for altitudes above 1000 ft, add 10 minutes for altitudes over 6000 ft).

Allow to cool overnight. Check all lids for a proper seal - it should have sucked down into vacuum seal, as it cooled.

Store properly sealed jars for later use, refrigerate any that did not seal, for use in the coming weeks.

*Corn Cob Jelly*

# "Corn Syrup"

Yes, the quotation marks are intentional. This isn't corn syrup in the traditional sense - you wouldn't want to use this in candy making, for instance.

No, this is a mildly corn flavoured, thick simple syrup that is great over sweet corn pancakes, drizzled over ice cream, used in cocktails - have some fun with it!

Makes about 5 cups

| | | |
|---|---|---|
| Corn cobs, kernels removed | 5 | 5 |
| Water | 6 cups | 1500 ml |
| Granulated sugar | 6 cups | 1500 ml |
| Salt | 1 tsp | 5 ml |

Chop up the stripped corn cobs into 1" chunks, place into a large pot. Cover with the water, bring to a boil, reduce heat and simmer for about 30 minutes (Liquid should be reduced to about half of the starting volume).

Remove corn cob pieces from the water, discard. Strain corn mixture through a wire sieve, into a clean bowl. Rinse pot and sieve out with cool water. Line sieve with at least 2 layers of cheesecloth, strain corn liquid through cheesecloth, back into the rinsed pot. Add sugar and salt, stir well.

Bring mixture back up to a boil, reduce heat slightly, and keep at a low boil for another 10 minutes. Remove from heat, allow to cool to room temperature. Transfer syrup to a bottle or jar, cover with a well-fitting lid. Store in the fridge for up to 3 months.

As the syrup ages, you may find that it will begin to recrystallize. If this happens, heat it up and add a tablespoon of water, stirring until it goes back to a smooth, syrupy consistency.

*"Corn Syrup"*

# Creamy Corn Dressing

If you're a fan of corn, and a fan of creamy dressings... this is a great salad dressing for you!

This combines the flavours of a traditional ranch dressing, with the addition of fresh, sweet corn - a perfect marriage!

Makes about 2 ½ cups of dressing

| | | |
|---|---|---|
| Ears fresh sweet corn, husks removed | 2 | 2 |
| Garlic clove, peeled and pressed | 1 | 1 |
| Milk | ½-3/4 cup | 125-175 ml |
| Apple cider vinegar | 1 tsp | 5 ml |
| Mayonnaise | 3/4 cup | 175 ml |
| Sour cream | ½ cup | 125 ml |
| Fresh dill weed | 1/4 cup | 50 ml |
| Fresh parsley | 1/4 cup | 50 ml |
| Finely chopped fresh chives | 2 tsp | 10 ml |
| Green onion, finely chopped | 1 | 1 |
| Pepper | ½-1 tsp | 2-5 ml |
| Cayenne pepper | 1/4 tsp | 1 ml |
| Salt | | |

Using a sharp knife, carefully cut kernels off the ears of corn. Place corn kernels in a blender or food processor, along with garlic, ½ cup of milk, and the apple cider vinegar. Process until corn is very smooth - around 2 minutes.

Add mayonnaise and sour cream, process until smooth and fully incorporated. Add dill, parsley, chives, green onion, pepper and cayenne, process for another 3 seconds. Season with salt to taste.

Chill for at least 30 minutes before serving, to allow the flavours to mix. Before serving, check the consistency, thinning with additional buttermilk if necessary.

*Creamy Corn Dressing*

# Atol de Elote

This is a hot corn beverage that is popular in South America - with many regional variations.

"Atol" on its own refers to a hot corn drink, the "elote" refers to this one specifically being made with fresh corn, rather than with hominy.

This is usually served as a beverage, but - depending on how starchy the corn is - can be served as a hot, almost custardy pudding.

4 servings

| | | |
|---|---|---|
| Ears fresh sweet corn, husks removed | 6 | 6 |
| Milk, divided | 4 cups | 1 L |
| Granulated sugar | ½-1 cup | 125-250 ml |
| Cinnamon sticks (about 3-inch long) | 1-2 | 1-2 |
| Salt | 1/4 - ½ tsp | 1-2 ml |
| Ground cinnamon, optional | | |

Using a sharp knife, carefully cut kernels off the ears of corn. Place corn kernels in a blender or food processor, along with about half of the milk. Process until corn is very smooth - around 2 minutes.

Transfer corn puree to a medium sized pot, along with the remaining milk. Bring to a boil, stirring frequently. Remove from heat.

Strain corn mixture through a wire sieve, into a clean bowl. Rinse pot and sieve out with cool water. Line sieve with at least 3 layers of cheesecloth, strain corn liquid through cheesecloth, back into the pot.

Add sugar, cinnamon stick(s), and salt to corn liquid, stir until well combined. Bring back to almost a boil, turn heat down and allow to simmer for 5 minutes, stirring frequently.

Distribute hot atole into serving mugs, garnish with a small pinch of ground cinnamon.

*Atol de Elote*

*Sweet Corn Liqueur and Sweet Corn Creme Liqueur*

# Sweet Corn Liqueur

Corn liqueur may sound unusual, but it's actually a great way to preserve and enjoy the flavour of fresh sweet corn, picked at its peak.   Serve chilled or at room temperature.

| Ears fresh sweet corn, husks removed | 3 | 3 |
| --- | --- | --- |
| Water | 1 cup | 250 ml |
| Granulated sugar | 3/4 cup | 175 ml |
| Vodka or bourbon | 3/4- 1 cup | 175-250 ml |

Using a sharp knife, carefully cut kernels off the ears of corn. Place corn kernels in a blender or food processor, along with water. Process until corn is pureed.

Transfer corn puree to a medium saucepan. Over medium heat, cook mixture until almost boiling, stirring frequently.  Remove from heat, allow to steep for 5-10 minutes.

Strain corn mixture through a wire sieve, into a clean bowl.  Rinse pot and sieve out with cool water.

Line sieve with at least 3 layers of cheesecloth, strain corn liquid through cheesecloth a second time, back into the pot. Add sugar, stir until dissolved. Allow mixture to cool.

Once mixture is cool, add vodka, starting with 3/4 cup.  Stir until well combined. Taste, add more vodka if you so desire. Transfer liqueur to a clean bottle or jar, cover, and store in fridge for up to 3 weeks.

# Sweet Corn Creme Liqueur

Much like non-cream sweet corn liqueur, another great way to experience the sweet taste of corn in a whole other light - this time with milk fat! Sweet, creamy, and so very delicious!

| | | |
|---|---|---|
| Ears fresh sweet corn, husks removed | 3 | 3 |
| Heavy cream | 1 cup | 250 ml |
| Sweetened condensed milk | 14 oz | 300 ml |
| Vodka or bourbon | 1 ½ - 2 cups | 375-250 ml |

Using a sharp knife, carefully cut kernels off the ears of corn. Place corn kernels in a blender or food processor, along with heavy cream. Process until corn is pureed.

Transfer corn puree to a medium saucepan. Over medium heat, cook mixture until almost boiling, stirring frequently. Remove from heat, allow to steep for 5-10 minutes.

Strain corn mixture through a wire sieve, into a clean bowl. Rinse pot and sieve out with cool water.

Line sieve with at least 3 layers of cheesecloth, strain corn liquid through cheesecloth, back into the pot. Allow to cool to room temperature.

Add sweetened condensed milk to corn liquid, stir until well combined. Add vodka, starting with 1 ½ cups. Stir until well combined. Taste, add more vodka if you so desire.

Transfer liqueur to a clean bottle or jar, cover, and store in fridge for up to 3 weeks.

# Quick Sweet Corn Soda

Very easy to make, yet very versatile. This cooks up in just minutes, but can be used to make cream soda, to use in a soda machine, or just enjoyed as a quick soda mix, a little at a time.

| | | |
|---|---|---|
| Ears fresh sweet corn, husks removed | 3 | 3 |
| Water | 1 ½ cups | 375 ml |
| Granulated sugar | 2 cups | 500 ml |
| Carbonated water, Seltzer Water, etc | | |

Using a sharp knife, carefully cut kernels off the ears of corn. Place corn kernels in a blender or food processor, along with water. Process until corn is pureed.

Transfer corn puree to a medium saucepan. Over medium heat, cook mixture until almost boiling, stirring frequently. Reduce heat, simmer 5 more minutes. Remove from heat, allow to steep for 10 minutes.

Strain corn mixture through a wire sieve, into a clean bowl. Rinse pot and sieve out with cool water. Line sieve with at least 3 layers of cheesecloth, strain corn liquid through cheesecloth, back into the pot.

Add sugar to corn liquid. Cook over medium heat, stirring until completely dissolved. Remove from heat, allow to cool to room temperature. Transfer syrup to a clean bottle or jar, cover, and store in fridge for up to 3 weeks

To use:

- Measure about 3 Tbsp (45 ml) soda syrup into a tall glass, top with carbonated/seltzer water, and stir gently to combine.

- Soda syrup can be used in soda machines, in place of store bought syrups.

- To force carbonate it, if you have the equipment: Make 6-8x batch of syrup, for 5 gallon keg. Top with distilled water. Seal off keg and carbonate per your set up.

For Corn Cream Soda: Add 1 Tbsp (15 ml) vanilla extract to cooled syrup before storing, stir well to combine.

*Sweet Corn Soda*

# Brewed Sweet Corn Soda

If you yearn for the taste of brewed sodas, this is a unique recipe for you. Takes a bit more commitment than the preceding recipe, but produces the characteristic flavours of old fashioned, brewed soda.

| | | |
|---|---|---|
| Ears fresh sweet corn, husks removed | 2 | 2 |
| Water | 3/4 cup | 175 ml |
| Granulated sugar | 1 cup | 250 ml |
| Bread yeast | 1/4 tsp | 1 ml |
| Water, room temperature* | 8 cups | 2 L |

Using a sharp knife, carefully cut kernels off the ears of corn. Place corn kernels in a blender or food processor, along with water. Process until corn is pureed. Transfer corn puree to a medium saucepan. Over medium heat, cook mixture until almost boiling, stirring frequently. Reduce heat, simmer 5 more minutes. Remove from heat, allow to steep for 10 minutes.

Strain corn mixture through a wire sieve, into a clean bowl. Rinse pot and sieve out with cool water. Line sieve with at least 3 layers of cheesecloth, strain corn liquid through cheesecloth, back into the pot. Add sugar to corn liquid. Cook over medium heat, stirring until completely dissolved. Remove from heat, allow to cool for 5 minutes or so.

Use a funnel to transfer cooled soda syrup to a clean 2L pop bottle. Add yeast and about 1 cup of water to the bottle, swirl to combine. Top with remaining water, leaving about 1" empty head space in the bottle. Cap tightly.

Allow bottle to sit at room temperature for 1-3 days, just until the bottle gets hard (pressurized!) from the carbonation that is building inside.

Chill pressurized bottle upright in the fridge for a few days, allowing the yeast to settle on the bottom of the bottle.

To serve, gentle pour from the bottle, taking care not to disturb the settled yeast. When you get down to the last bit of soda in the bottle, discard it along with the yeast.

* Use distilled or otherwise bottled water - tap water can impart weird flavours on the finished drink.

For Corn Cream Soda:  Add ½ - 1 Tbsp (7-15 ml) vanilla extract to cooled syrup before adding yeast, stir well to combine.

# Corn Cob Wine

Yes, you read that right - corn cob wine. While this recipe has its roots in prohibition-era underground brewing - and can be considered fairly trashy! - this produces a uniquely flavoured, sweet homemade wine. If you're like my husband and I - Homebrewers who will wander a grocery store and think "Can we ferment that?" - this is a cool little recipe to try. The answer is "yes", by the way - and it's delicious!

Per Gallon:

| | | |
|---|---|---|
| Ears fresh sweet corn, husks removed | 6 | 6 |
| Spring water | 1 gallon | 4 L |
| Granulated sugar | 9 cups | 2 1/4 L |
| Yeast nutrient | 1 tsp | 5 ml |
| Acid blend | ½ tsp | 2 ml |

1 packet of wine yeast*
*We like Red Star "Cote de Blancs" for this recipe)

2 x 1 gallon glass carboys & stoppers, 1 air lock, siphon, siphon tubing, wine bottles, corks

Using a sharp knife, carefully cut kernels off the ears of corn. In batches, place corn kernels in a blender or food processor, along with ~1/2 cup water. Process until corn is pureed, transfer to a large pot, along with the stripped cobs of corn and sugar. Heat to almost boiling, stirring until sugar is dissolved. Simmer gently for 25 minutes, remove from heat, stir in yeast nutrient and acid blend. Cover with sanitized pot lid, allow to cool to room temperature.

Once mixture has cooled, use a sanitized funnel to transfer cooled mixture to a sanitized 1 gallon glass carboy. Sprinkle yeast into carboy, cover with sanitized air lock. Let sit, undisturbed, overnight. Within 48 hours, you should notice fermentation activity – bubbles in the airlock, carbonation and /or swirling in the liquid. This means you're good to go! Put the carboy somewhere cool (not cold!), and leave it alone for a month or so.

Using sanitized equipment, rack the clarified wine off the sediment, into a clean, freshly sanitized 1 gallon carboy. Cap with sanitized airlock, leave it alone for another 2-3 months.

When you've let it clarify as much as you have patience for – with no more sediment being produced – you can move on to bottling. Using sanitized equipment, rack the wine into clean, sanitized wine bottles, and cap them. Allow to age for a month or so before drinking.

*Corn Cob Wine*

125

*Sweet Corn Pudding*

# Desserts

## Sweet Corn Pudding

Such a simple dessert, pudding is a great way to showcase the familiar flavour of sweet corn. Serve this warm or chilled - warm corn pudding is a truly unique comfort food!

Makes 4 cups of pudding

| Ears fresh sweet corn, husks removed | 3 | 3 |
| --- | --- | --- |
| Whole milk | 3 cups | 750 ml |
| Granulated sugar | ½ cup | 125 ml |
| Cornstarch | 1/4 cup | 50 ml |
| Salt | 1/4 tsp | 1 ml |
| Butter | 2 Tbsp | 30 ml |

Using a sharp knife, carefully cut kernels off the ears of corn, placing them into blender or food processor, along with 2 cups of the milk. Blitz until fairly smooth.

Pour corn mixture into a medium saucepan, and bring just to a simmer over medium heat. Turn heat down to low, allow to simmer for 5 minutes. Once 5 minutes have passed, remove from heat and allow to steep for 20 minutes.

Once mixture has steeped, run it through a fine mesh strainer twice, ending up back in the saucepan. Discard corn pulp. Add sugar to the corn milk, heat to just to a simmer, stirring occasionally.

Meanwhile, whisk together remaining milk, cornstarch, and salt until smooth. Pour into the hot milk, whisking constantly to incorporate. Continue to whisk over medium heat until mixture is thick, and coats the back of a spoon, being careful to not allow it to boil. Remove from heat, stir in butter, and pour into serving dishes. Chill completely before serving.

Variations:

- Melt 8 oz white chocolate, stir into pudding along with the butter.
- Substitute coconut cream for half of the milk

# Sweet Corn Creme Brulee

A unique variation on a very traditional dessert. The crunch of the sugar crust is the perfect foil for the creamy goodness of the corn flavoured custard.

Makes 6 small Creme Brulees

| | | |
|---|---|---|
| Large egg yolks | 8 | 8 |
| Granulated sugar | 1/4 cup | 50 ml |
| Heavy cream | 2 cups | 500 ml |
| Ears fresh sweet corn, husks removed | 2-3 | 2-3 |
| Granulated sugar | 1/4 cup | 50 ml |

Preheat oven to 325°F  (160°C)

Combine egg yolks and 1/4 cup sugar together in a bowl, whisking until the mixture becomes thick and pale yellow. Add ½ cup of the heavy cream, whisking until incorporated and smooth. Set aside.

Using a sharp knife, carefully cut kernels off the ears of corn, placing them into blender or food processor.  Blitz until corn is well chopped up, add remaining heavy cream, and blitz JUST until smooth - you don't want to turn it into whipped cream.

Heat corn and liquid mixture to just to a simmer, stirring occasionally. Do not let it come to boil! Remove from heat, allow to steep for 10 minutes.

Once mixture has steeped, run it through a fine mesh strainer, and into a clean saucepan.  Discard the corn pulp. Heat mixture over medium just to a simmer once again.

Remove from heat. Slowly drizzle hot cream mixture into the egg mixture, whisking constantly. Pour into 6 ramekins or custard cups, and arrange in a large pan. Carefully add water to the large pan, till about halfway up the sides of the ramekins.

Bake until custard is set, but wiggles in the middle - about 45-50 minutes.

Remove from oven, allow to cool to room temperature, and then chill for at least 2 hours.   When ready to serve, sprinkle 2-3 tsp (10-15 ml)  sugar evenly over each custard. Use a small, hand held kitchen torch to melt sugar.

Serve immediately.

*Sweet Corn Creme Brulee*

# Sweet Corn Flan

Much like with the creme brulee, the flan is a great way to incorporate sweet corn flavour into an elegant dessert.   With the popularity of flan as a Latin-American dessert, I think it's especially fitting to make a corn flavoured version - given the origins of the grain!   Serves about 8

| | | |
|---|---|---|
| Ears fresh sweet corn, husks removed | 2-3 | 2-3 |
| Milk | 2 cups | 500 ml |
| Heavy cream | 2 cups | 500 ml |
| Granulated sugar | 2 cups | 500 ml |
| Water | 1/4 cup | 50 ml |
| Large eggs | 9 | 9 |
| Granulated sugar | ½ cup | 125 ml |

Preheat oven to 275°F (140°C).  Generously grease a flan pan, quiche dish or glass baking dish

Using a sharp knife, carefully cut kernels off the ears of corn, placing them into blender or food processor along with the milk.  Blitz until corn is well chopped up, add heavy cream, and blitz JUST until smooth - you don't want to turn it into whipped cream!

Pour corn mixture into a medium saucepan, and bring just to a simmer over medium heat.  Turn heat down to low, allow to simmer for 5 minutes.  Once 5 minutes have passed, remove from heat and allow to steep for 20 minutes. Once mixture has steeped, run it through a fine mesh strainer, and into a mixing bowl.  Set aside.

Combine 2 cups  of the sugar with water in a small saucepan over medium heat. Cook until sugar is a light golden brown, about 15 - 20 minutes.  Pour into prepared baking dish.

In a separate mixing bowl, combine eggs and sugar, beating until well blended, pale, and smooth. Add corn / cream mixture  a little at a time, stirring until fully incorporated and smooth. Slowly and carefully pour over the caramel in the flan pan.  Place flan pan into a larger baking pan. Carefully add water to the large pan, till about halfway up the sides of the flan pan. Bake for 45 - 60 minutes (depends on how deep your pan is!) or until custard is set. Remove from oven, cool to room temperature, then chill completely.

To serve, run a knife around the outside edge of the flan to loosen. Place a serving plate - face down -  over the baking dish, and carefully invert.

*Sweet Corn Flan*

# Sweet Corn Panna Cotta

Steeping dairy ingredients with fresh sweet corn provides the base of a wide variety of creamy desserts - the ideal way to show off the subtle, sweet flavour of the grain. One of the most simple to make is panna cotta - this one produces a beautiful, pale yellow dessert, with the clear flavour of corn shining through!

Makes about 4 servings

| Unflavoured gelatin powder | 1 ½ tsp | 7 ml |
| Cold water | 3 Tbsp | 45 ml |
| Ears fresh sweet corn, husk removed | 2-3 | 2-3 |
| Milk | 3/4 cup | 175 ml |
| Heavy cream | 1 cup | 250 ml |
| Granulated sugar | ½ cup | 125 ml |
| Sour cream | ½ cup | 125 ml |

Sprinkle the gelatin over the cold water in a small bowl and allow to absorb for five minutes.

Using a sharp knife, carefully cut kernels off the ears of corn, placing them into a food processor or blender, along with the milk. Process until corn is rendered into small pieces. Pour into a saucepan, along with heavy cream.

Heat corn and liquid mixture to just to a simmer, stirring occasionally. Do not let it come to boil! Remove from heat, allow to steep for 10 minutes.

Once mixture has steeped, run it through a fine mesh strainer, and into a clean saucepan, along with the sugar. Discard the corn pulp. Heat mixture over medium just to a simmer once again, stirring until sugar dissolves. Meanwhile, microwave the gelatin for about 15 seconds, or until it's melted.

Once the milk mixture has come to a simmer, remove it from the heat. Whisk in the gelatin until fully incorporated, and the mixture is smooth. Add sour cream, whisking once again till fully incorporated and smooth. Pour into four greased ramekins or custard cups. Chill for at least 2 hours until set.

Top with glazed nuts, candied bacon, blueberry sauce, or salted caramel sauce - recipes start on page 142.

*Sweet Corn Panna Cotta*

133

# Sweet Corn Ice Cream

This recipe is actually for a frozen custard, more so than an ice cream - but the lines between the two have really blurred, in modern usage . Nonetheless, this dessert is becoming popular at summer festivals and other events - a far cry from how bizarre people seemed to take the idea when I created this recipe back in 2006!

Makes about 1 ½ quarts

| Ears fresh sweet corn, husks removed | 3 | 3 |
| Whole milk | 2 cups | 500 ml |
| Large egg yolks | 8 | 8 |
| Granulated sugar | 3/4 cup | 175 ml |
| Heavy cream | 2 cups | 500 ml |
| Salt | 1/4 tsp | 1 ml |

Using a sharp knife, carefully cut kernels off the ears of corn, placing them into a food processor or blender, along with the milk. Process until corn is rendered into small pieces. Pour into a saucepan.

Heat corn and milk mixture to just to a simmer, stirring occasionally. Do not let it come to boil! Remove from heat, allow to steep for 10 minutes.

Once mixture has steeped, run it through a fine mesh strainer, and into a clean saucepan. Discard the corn pulp. Heat mixture over medium just to a simmer once again.

Combine egg yolks and sugar in a medium mixing bowl. Whisk until fluffy, pale yellow, and smooth. Add heavy cream and salt, whisk until well incorporated.

Stream egg mixture into saucepan, whisking to incorporate. Cook over medium heat, stirring constantly, until mixture thickens - it should be thick enough to coat the back of a spoon. Remove from heat, cool to room temperature, and then chill thoroughly until ready to use.

Follow your ice cream maker's instructions to freeze custard mixture - depending on the size of the ice cream maker, you may need to do this in multiple batches. Keep any extra ice cream mix chilled until use - process into frozen custard within a day or two.

Serve immediately for a soft ice cream, or freeze for at least 2 hours for a more firm ice cream.

*Sweet Corn Ice Cream*

# Sweet Corn Frozen Pops

Frozen pops are always a fun way to cool down in the summertime... and that goes double when incorporating fresh seasonal flavours and bright colours!

These sweet corn frozen pops are tasty on their own, but really shine with the addition of fresh fruit.  Use blueberries, sliced strawberries, chopped up fresh ripe peaches - the sweet corn base works wonderfully with almost any kind of fruit!

The number of servings this produces will depend on the size of the pop molds that you're using, whether you're adding fruit, and how much fruit you're using, if so. Feel free to double - or half! - the recipe as needed.

Makes about 4 cups of liquid to freeze

| | | |
|---|---|---|
| Ears fresh sweet corn, husks removed | 4 | 4 |
| Coconut milk | 4 cups | 1 L |
| Granulated sugar | 1/4- ½ cup | 50-125 ml |
| Salt | 1/4 tsp | 1 ml |

Using a sharp knife, carefully cut kernels off the ears of corn, placing them into blender or food processor. Add coconut milk, blitz until corn is well chopped up.

Pour corn and coconut milk mixture into a medium saucepan., and bring just to a simmer over medium heat.  Turn heat down to low, allow to simmer for 10 minutes. Once 10 minutes have passed, remove from heat and allow to steep for 30 minutes.

Once mixture has steeped, run it through a fine mesh strainer, and into a mixing bowl, along with 1/4 cup of the sugar, and salt. Stir well, taste for sweetness - adding more sugar if you like - and allow to cool completely.  Pour mixture into popsicle molds of your choice, set up and freeze according to manufacturer's directions.

**Variations:**

Fruit:   If using fruit, place fruit into molds before pouring liquid in

Milk:   You can use almond milk, cashew milk, cow's milk, half and half, or whatever milk substitute you like - you just may want to adjust the sweetener based on what you use.

Sweetener:   You can swap out the sugar for honey, or even a sugar substitute, if needed.

*Sweet Corn Frozen Pops*

*Easy White Chocolate Sweet Corn Fudge*

# Easy White Chocolate Sweet Corn Fudge

Not the most elegant dish ever, but a quick and easy way to get your sweet corn fix, in dessert form!

| | | |
|---|---|---|
| Ears fresh sweet corn, husks removed | 2 | 2 |
| White chocolate chips | 4 cups | 1000 ml |
| Salt | Pinch | Pinch |

Before getting started, line an 8" square pan with parchment paper, or grease generously with butter.

Using a sharp knife, carefully cut kernels off the ear of corn. Measure out 2/3 cup of kernels, place them into a blender or food processor, and puree until as smooth as possible.

Combine white chocolate chips and pureed corn in a saucepan. Cook over medium-low heat, stirring frequently until chocolate melts and mixture is smooth. (Alternatively, combine in a microwave safe bowl and nuke for 30 second intervals, stirring between each, until chocolate is melted and mixture is smooth). Remove from heat, stir in salt. Spread into prepared pan, chill until set.

# Sweet Corn Cheesecake

As you read earlier, corn can make a fantastic cheesecake. Not only does it work for the savoury version in the main dishes chapter, it works very well in a sweeter, dessert version!

| | | |
|---|---|---|
| Ears fresh corn, husks removed | 3 | 3 |
| Heavy cream | 2 cups | 500 ml |
| Cream cheese, room temperature | 2 lbs | 1 Kg |
| Granulated sugar | 1 ½ cups | 375 ml |
| Sour cream | 1 cup | 250 ml |
| Large eggs | 6 | 6 |
| Lemon, juice of | 1 | 1 |
| 1 cheesecake crust, next page | | |

Preheat oven to 350 F   (180 C)

Using a sharp knife, carefully cut kernels off the ears of corn, placing them into blender or food processor.  Blitz until corn is well chopped up, add heavy cream, and blitz JUST until smooth - you don't want to turn it into whipped cream!

Pour corn mixture into a medium saucepan, and bring just to a simmer over medium heat. Turn heat down to low, allow to simmer for 5 minutes. Once 5 minutes have passed, remove from heat and allow to steep for 20 minutes.

Once mixture has steeped, run it through a fine mesh strainer, and into a mixing bowl. Allow to cool to room temperature.

In stand mixer, beat together cream cheese and sugar until smooth. Add sour cream, eggs, and lemon juice. Beat on low / medium-low until smooth. Add corn mixture, beat on low just until combined. Gently pour batter into prepared crust. Chill for 10 minutes.

Bake for 15 minutes. After 15 minutes, turn the oven down to 325 F (160 C) and bake for 50 minutes. Once baking time is complete, turn off the oven and allow cake to cool - WITHOUT opening the door! - for 2 hours. Chill cake thoroughly before serving.

Serve plain, or top with glazed nuts, candied bacon, blueberry sauce, or salted caramel sauce - recipes start on page 142.


# Basic Cheesecake Crust

| Crumbs * | 1 ½ cup | 375 ml |
| Granulated sugar | 1/4 cup | 50 ml |
| Butter, melted | 5 Tbsp | 75 ml |

Combine all ingredients until completely incorporated & moistened. Evenly distribute across the bottom of a 9"spring form pan.

Press ingredients firmly into pan, extending crust partway up the sides of the pan. Chill for at least 1 hour.

* Crumbs:

- Use graham cracker crumbs for a basic, traditional cheesecake crust.
- Oreos, Nilla wafers, or any other type of dry cookie can be used to customize crust flavour.
- Substitute finely chopped nuts for all or part of the crumbs.

*Sweet Corn Cheesecake*

141

# Candied Bacon Dessert Topping

Use as much bacon as you think you'll need, and enough brown sugar to coat it!

Bacon (Ideally thick cut!)
Brown Sugar

Preheat oven to 325 F (160 C),  line a baking sheet with parchment paper. In a large mixing bowl, coat bacon slices with brown sugar. Arrange bacon on baking sheet, sprinkle with additional brown sugar.  Bake for 25-30 minutes, or until desired level of crispy. Allow to cool slightly, then crumble.

# Salted Caramel Sauce

Salted caramel has been a popular flavour in the past few years, being used for almost any kind of dessert imaginable. The rich flavour of the caramel, with a bite of saltiness works really well as a foil to the creamy, corny desserts early in his chapter. This sauce keeps well in the fridge, and should be good for around 2.5-3 weeks- just warm and stir before serving. Be absolutely sure that your butter and cream are at room temperature, or even a bit warmer - adding these as cold ingredients to the caramel can cause it to seize and turn into a crystallized mess. Makes about 3 cups

| | | |
|---|---|---|
| Granulated sugar | 2 cups | 500 ml |
| Corn syrup | 1/4 cup | 50 ml |
| Butter, room temperature | 1 ½ cups | 375 ml |
| Heavy cream, room temperature | 1 cup | 250 ml |
| Sea salt | 1 Tbsp | 15 ml |

In a large pot combine sugar and corn syrup, bringing to a boil over medium-high heat.  Gently stir the mixture just until the sugar dissolves, trying not to splash much of it up the sides of the pot. Once the sugar as dissolved, turn the heat down to medium and stop stirring - just swirl the pan gently, every once in a while as it cooks.

Use a candy thermometer to keep an eye on the temperature of the caramel as it begins to turn golden brown.  Once it reaches 350 F (180 C), remove pan from heat and carefully stir in the butter - the mixture will bubble up somewhat violently at this point!  Continue stirring until all of the butter is melted and fully incorporated into the sugar mix.

Once butter is incorporated, slowly and carefully pour the cream into the pot, knowing that it will once again bubble up. Stir well, until cream is completely incorporated, leaving you with a thick, smooth sauce. Mix in the sea salt, allow to cool for 20 minutes or so. Pour sauce into a glass jar(s) and allow to cool to room temperature before covering with a lid.

*Dessert Toppings*

# Blueberry Sauce

This sauce is particularly great served over sweet corn ice cream, or layered with sweet corn mousse for a unique and beautiful parfait!  Makes about 2 cups

| Fresh blueberries | 1 pint | 500 ml |
|---|---|---|
| Granulated sugar | 3/4 cup | 175 ml |
| Water | 2/3 cup | 150 ml |
| Fresh lemon juice | 2 tsp | 10 ml |
| Vanilla extract | ½ - 1 tsp | 2-5 ml |

Combine blueberries, sugar, water, and lemon juice in a medium saucepan. Bring to a boil, stirring frequently.  Turn temperature down and simmer until the blueberries have broken down into a thick sauce, about 20 minutes. Remove from heat, cool to room temperature, before stirring in vanilla extract.  Transfer cooled blueberry sauce to a jar, chill until serving.

**Variations:**

- I love this with the zest of 1 orange mixed in with the first step.
- Try substituting Amaretto liqueur for all or part of the water - delicious!

# Glazed Nuts

While these nuts are great on their own as a dessert, they're also a perfect topping for many of the corn desserts featured in this chapter. I like to use cashews, walnuts, or pecans for use on corn recipes, but feel free to experiment.  You can use almonds, peanuts.. pretty much any type of nut you prefer. Use just one type, or a mix of your favorites!

| Nuts of choice | 1 lb | 500 g |
|---|---|---|
| Granulated sugar | 1 1/4 cup | 300 ml |
| Butter, melted | 3 Tbsp | 45 ml |

Line 2 baking sheets with parchment paper.

Combine nuts, sugar, and melted butter in a large, heavy pan.  Cook over medium heat, stirring frequently, until sugar melts, turns golden, and coats the nuts - this will take between 5-10 minutes.

Divide nuts between the two cookie sheets, spreading loosely across each. Allow the nuts to cool completely, store in an airtight container

# Sweet Corn Pastry Cream

Pastry Cream - also known as crème pâtissière - is a very thick, rich custard. It's used in many French pastries- such as eclairs and cream puffs- and also as filling for tarts and cakes. This recipe makes about 1 ½ cups of finished pastry cream - feel free to double or triple the recipe if needed.

| Ears fresh sweet corn, husks removed | 3 | 3 |
| Milk | 1 ½ cups | 375 ml |
| Large egg yolks | 3 | 3 |
| Granulated sugar | 1/4 cup | 50 ml |
| Corn starch | 1 Tbsp | 15 ml |
| Butter | 2 Tbsp | 30 ml |

Using a sharp knife, carefully cut kernels off the ears of corn, placing them into blender or food processor, along with milk. Blitz until corn is well chopped up and mixture is relatively smooth.

Pour corn mixture into a medium saucepan, and bring just to a simmer over medium heat. Turn heat down to low, allow to simmer for 5 minutes. Once 5 minutes have passed, remove from heat and allow to steep for 20 minutes.

Once mixture has steeped, run it through a fine mesh strainer, and into a mixing bowl, set aside.

In a separate bowl, whisk yolks together with sugar until fluffy and pale yellow. Add corn starch, whisk until incorporated and smooth. Set aside.

In a small saucepan, bring corn milk to a light boil. Measure about 1/4 cup of the hot milk liquid, and stream slowly into egg mixture while whisking. Continue streaming liquid and whisking until it is completely incorporated, and mixture is smooth. Repeat with another 1/4 cup (50 ml) of hot liquid.

Remove saucepan from heat, pour egg mixture into milk mixture, whisking constantly. Once fully incorporated and smooth, return to heat, turning heat down to low. Continue whisking mixture constantly, cooking until mixture is very thick. Remove from heat, whisk in butter until fully incorporated and smooth.

Cover with plastic wrap, chill until needed.

*Cream Puffs*

# Cream Puffs

Cream puffs are a great way to showcase your fresh corn pastry cream - and they are quite easy to make!  Cream puffs start out with the batter - Pâte à choux, or "choux pastry". It's a basic recipe that's used to make everything from cream puffs and eclairs to cruellers and churros. It doesn't contain any leavening ingredients (yeast, baking powder, baking soda, etc), instead relying on its high moisture content to puff during baking. Baked at a high temperature, the water becomes steam and creates large air pockets in the final product.

## Pâte à choux

| | | |
|---|---|---|
| Water | 1 cup | 250 ml |
| Butter | ½ cup | 125 ml |
| Granulated sugar | 1 tsp | 5 ml |
| Salt | ½ tsp | 2 ml |
| Flour | 1 cup | 250 ml |
| Large eggs | 3 | 3 |
| Egg whites | 2 | 2 |

Preheat oven to 425 F (220 C). Line a baking sheet with parchment paper or use a nonstick baking sheet. It's very important to not grease the pan - it will cause the pastries to flatten!

Combine water, butter, sugar, and salt in a medium sauce pan, heat to a boil. Remove from heat, add flour, stirring until well incorporated. Reduce heat to medium, return saucepan to stove top. Cook for another minute or so, until the dough comes together, leaving the sides of the pan. Transfer dough to the bowl of your mixer. Using the paddle attachment, beat the dough for a minute or so to allow it to cool slightly.

Meanwhile, beat together eggs and egg whites in a small bowl. With the mixer set to medium speed, add egg mixture to dough a little at a time, allowing eggs to fully incorporate into the dough before adding more. It may look like a separating mess, but I promise it will come together!  When all of the eggs are incorporated and the dough is smooth and shiny, it's ready to pipe!  It'll be soft and a bit sticky, but more or less be able to hold it's shape. Pipe it out according to your desired use (below), and bake for the time indicated.

**Cream Puffs**:

Using a pastry bag with a medium/ large round or star tip, pipe out rounds that are about 2-2.5" in diameter and 1 ½" tall, leaving 2-3" between mounds.. Use a moistened finger to pat down any peaks of dough that may form as you finish piping each.

Bake for 12 minutes, then -WITHOUT opening the oven door - turn the temperature down to 350 F (180 C) and bake for another 35 minutes.  Crack the oven door open a few inches, turn the heat off, and allow the puffs to cool in the oven for 30 minutes. This step allows the insides to dry out, providing a stronger structure to prevent collapse.

Once puffs are completely cool, cut in half horizontally, and fill with pastry cream, dust with powdered sugar, drizzle with white chocolate corn glaze, and/or serve with fresh fruit or berries!

**Profiteroles:**

Using spoons or a pastry bags, make tablespoon-sized mounds of batter, leaving 2" of space between each. Use a moistened finger to pat down any peaks of dough that may form as you finish piping each.

Bake for 12 minutes, then -WITHOUT opening the oven door - turn the temperature down to 350 F (180 C) and bake for another 25 minutes.  Crack the oven door open a few inches, turn the heat off, and allow the puffs to cool in the oven for 30 minutes. This step allows the insides to dry out, providing a stronger structure to prevent collapse.

Fill a pastry bag with your choice of pastry cream, pudding, or mousse.  Once puffs are completely cool, jam the tip of the pastry bag into the side of a puff, and fill! Dust with powdered sugar, or drizzle with white chocolate corn glaze, page 149.

**Eclairs:**

Using a pastry bag with a large round or star tip, pipe out logs that are about 2" x 5-6" leaving 2" between logs. Use a moistened finger to pat down any peaks of dough that may form as you finish piping each.

Bake for 12 minutes, then -WITHOUT opening the oven door - turn the temperature down to 350 F (180 C) and bake for another 30 minutes.  Crack the oven door open a few inches, turn the heat off, and allow the puffs to cool in the oven for 30 minutes. This step allows the insides to dry out, providing a stronger structure to prevent collapse.

Once logs are completely cool, cut in half horizontally, and fill with your choice of pastry cream, pudding, or mousse.  Dip the tops in white chocolate corn glaze, chill.

**Mini Eclairs:**

Using a pastry bag with a medium/ large round or star tip, pipe out logs that are about 1" x 2" leaving 2" between logs. Use a moistened finger to pat down any peaks of dough that may form as you finish piping each.

Bake for 12 minutes, then - WITHOUT opening the oven door - turn the temperature down to 350 F  (180 C) and bake for another 20 minutes.  Crack the oven door open a few inches, turn the heat off, and allow the puffs to cool in the oven for 30 minutes. This step allows the insides to dry out, providing a stronger structure to prevent collapse.

Fill a pastry bag with your choice of pastry cream, pudding, or mousse.  Once puffs are completely cool, jam the tip of the pastry bag into the side of a puff, and fill! Dip the tops in white chocolate corn glaze, chill.

# White Chocolate Corn Glaze

| | | |
|---|---|---|
| Ear fresh sweet corn, husks removed | 1 | 1 |
| Heavy cream | ½ cup | 125 ml |
| White chocolate | 6 oz | 170 g |

Using a sharp knife, carefully cut kernels off the ears of corn, placing them into blender or food processor.  Blitz until corn is well chopped up and relatively smooth. Pour corn mixture into a medium saucepan along with the cream, and bring just to a simmer over medium heat.  Turn heat down to low, allow to simmer for 5 minutes.  Once 5 minutes have passed, remove from heat and allow to steep for 20 minutes.

Finely chop white chocolate, place into a glass or metal mixing bowl, and set aside.

Once corn mixture has steeped, run it through a fine mesh strainer twice, ending with the mixture back in the pot. Discard the corn pulp.  Heat corn cream to a boil, remove from heat. Pour hot cream into the bowl of white chocolate. Let sit for 3-5 minutes. Starting in the middle of the bowl, slowly start stirring the chocolate and cream until all of the chocolate is melted and  the cream has disappeared into it – it should be smooth.

Glaze can be made a day or two in advance and kept - covered - in the refrigerator. Warm in the microwave for 20-30 seconds when ready to use.

# White Chocolate Sweet Corn Truffles

Seeing the prices for commercially produced truffles, many seem to think that they are much more labor intensive and specialized than they actually are.  Here is a quick and easy recipe for my sweet corn truffles - unique, delicious, and elegant!

| | | |
|---|---|---|
| Ears fresh sweet corn, husks removed | 3 | 3 |
| Good quality white chocolate chips | 12 oz | 375 g |
| Heavy cream | ½ cup | 125 ml |
| Butter | 2 Tbsp | 30 ml |
| Powdered/confectioners/icing sugar | | |

Using a sharp knife, carefully cut kernels off the ears of corn, placing them into blender or food processor.  Blitz until corn is well chopped up and relatively smooth.

Pour corn mixture into a medium saucepan along with the cream, and bring just to a simmer over medium heat.  Turn heat down to low, allow to simmer for 5 minutes. Once 5 minutes have passed, remove from heat and allow to steep for 20 minutes.

Finely chop white chocolate, place into a glass or metal mixing bowl, and set aside.

Once corn mixture has steeped, run it through a fine mesh strainer.  Measure out ½ cup liquid, discard any extra liquid.  Run through the strainer one more time, ending with the mixture back in the pot. Discard the corn pulp, add butter to the pot.

Heat corn cream to a boil, remove from heat. Pour hot cream mixture into the bowl of white chocolate. Let sit for 3-5 minutes. Starting in the middle of the bowl, slowly start stirring the chocolate and cream until all of the chocolate is melted and the cream has disappeared into it – it should be smooth.

Cover with plastic wrap, preferably resting right on top of the surface – this prevents a skin from forming while it cools. Chill in the fridge for at least an hour or two, until it's pretty solid. Once solid, scoop out small amounts (a teaspoon or two), and roll them into balls. Try to handle the chocolate as quickly as possible, or it will melt.

Once all of the ganache is rolled into balls: wash and dry hands, then roll ganache centers in powdered sugar. Store in an airtight container for up to 1 week.

*Sweet Corn Truffles*

*Sweet Corn Mousse*

# Sweet Corn Mousse

When it comes to mousse, there are two main styles - "Traditional" and "Easy". Traditional mousse is made with raw egg yolks and/or egg whites.  While this is perfectly safe for the vast majority of the population, pregnant women, the elderly, and immune compromised
individuals may want to opt for the Easy version, which does not contain any raw eggs.

# Easy Sweet Corn  Mousse

Makes 2-4 servings

| | | |
|---|---|---|
| Ears fresh sweet corn, husks removed | 2-3 | 2-3 |
| Heavy cream | 2 cups | 500 ml |
| Granulated sugar | 1/3 cup | 75 ml |
| Unflavoured gelatin powder | 1 ½ tsp | 7 ml |
| Cold water | 1/3 cup | 75 ml |

Using a sharp knife, carefully cut kernels off the ears of corn, placing them into blender or food processor.  Blitz until corn is well chopped up, add heavy cream, and blitz JUST until smooth - you don't want to turn it into whipped cream... yet!

Heat corn and liquid mixture to just to a simmer, stirring occasionally. Do not let it come to boil! Remove from heat, allow to steep for 10 minutes.

Once mixture has steeped, run it through a fine mesh strainer, and into a clean mixing bowl. Add sugar to warm mixture, stirring until dissolved.  Cover, allow to cool to room temperature, then chill until very cold.

In a small bowl, sprinkle gelatin over water and allow to soak for 5 minutes. Transfer bowl to microwave, heat in 10 second increments until gelatin dissolves into the water.

Remove corn liquid from the fridge. Whip until stiff peaks form, then carefully fold in the gelatin mixture, stirring until combined.

Pour into 2-4 serving glasses, chill until set, about 2 hours.

# Traditional Sweet Corn Mousse

Serves 2-4

| | | |
|---|---|---|
| Ears fresh sweet corn, husks removed | 2-3 | 2-3 |
| Heavy cream | 1 cup | 250 ml |
| Granulated sugar | 1/4 cup | 50 ml |
| Large egg yolks | 2 | 2 |
| Large egg whites | 3 | 3 |

Using a sharp knife, carefully cut kernels off the ears of corn, placing them into blender or food processor.  Blitz until corn is well chopped up, add heavy cream, and blitz JUST until smooth - you don't want to turn it into whipped cream.

Heat corn and cream mixture to just to a simmer, stirring occasionally. Do not let it come to boil! Remove from heat, allow to steep for 10 minutes.

Once mixture has steeped, run it through a fine mesh strainer, and into a clean mixing bowl. Discard the corn pulp.  Cover bowl with plastic wrap, chill well - at least 1 hour.

Combine sugar and egg yolks together, beat until pale yellow and fluffy. Stir in heavy cream mixture a little at a time, until fully incorporated. Whip until stiff peaks form, transfer to fridge.

In a separate bowl, whip the egg whites until stiff peaks form. Carefully fold in chilled whipped cream mixture, stirring until combined.

Pour into 2-4 serving glasses, chill until set, about 2 hours.

# Gluten-Free Adjustments

While the vast majority of the recipes in this book are inherently gluten-free, a few will take adjustments to become gluten-free recipes.

Breakfast Corn Muffins, Page 21:

Omit all-purpose flour. Mix together ½ cup light buckwheat flour, and 1/4 cup each of sorghum flour, tapioca starch, and masa flour, add this mixture when the recipe calls for the all-purpose flour.

Sweet Corn Pancakes, Page 22:

Omit all-purpose flour. Mix together 2/3 cup light buckwheat flour and 1/3 cup sorghum flour, add this mixture when the recipe calls for the all-purpose flour.

Buttermilk Corn Scones, Page 24:

Omit all-purpose flour. Mix together 1 cup light buckwheat flour, 3/4 cup millet flour, 1/4 cup potato flour, and 2 tsp tapioca starch, add this mixture when the recipe calls for the all-purpose flour. Increase baking powder to 3 tsp, increase buttermilk to 1 1/4 cups

Corn, Kale, and Bacon Strata, Page 32:

Use gluten-free bread instead of a baguette. You'll need about 2 loaves.

Sweet Corn Quiche, Page 34:

Use a prepared gluten-free frozen pie crust. Alternately, make your own, with our quiche recipe in Beyond Flour 2.

Breakfast Burritos, Page 38:

Use gluten-free flour or corn tortillas. Alternately, we do have a great recipe for gluten-free flour tortillas in "Beyond Flour", and a fabulous flour-corn hybrid tortilla in "Beyond Flour 2".

Sweet Corn Fritters, Page 40:  Omit all-purpose flour. Mix together 2/3 cup light buckwheat flour and 1/4 cup white rice flour, add this mixture when the recipe calls for the all-purpose flour. Allow batter to rest for 10 minutes before frying.

Beer Battered Corn on the Cob, Page 45:  Omit all-purpose flour. Mix together 2/3 cup masa flour, 1/4 cup white rice flour, and 3/4 tsp xanthan gum, add this mixture when the recipe calls for the all-purpose flour.

Scalloped Corn, Page 56:  Use gluten-free crackers instead of Ritz or Club crackers

Sweet Corn Bruschetta, Page 66:  Use gluten-free bread instead of a baguette.

Roasted Corn Bread, Page 68:  Omit all-purpose flour. Mix together ½ cup light buckwheat flour, 1/3 cup masa, 1/3 cup sorghum flour, and 1/4 cup tapioca starch, add this mixture when the recipe calls for the all-purpose flour.

Midwest Goes Southwest Hot Dish, Page 82:  Make sure to use a gluten-free condensed soup

Corn and Cottage Pie, Page 86:  Omit all-purpose flour, use ½ cup corn or potato starch in place of it. Use gluten-free puff pastry sheets - these can be hard to find, though.

Grilled Corn Quesadillas, Page 94:  Use gluten-free flour or corn tortillas. Alternately, we do have a great recipe for gluten-free flour tortillas in "Beyond Flour", and a fabulous flour-corn hybrid tortilla in "Beyond Flour 2".

Sweet Corn Cheesecake, Page 139:  Use nuts or gluten-free cookies for the crust recipe.

Cream Puffs, Page 147:  Omit all-purpose flour. Mix together 1/3 cup each of sweet rice flour, white rice flour, and millet flour, 1 tsp xanthan gum, and ½ tsp of baking powder, add this mixture when the recipe calls for the all-purpose flour.

# Conversions

To accommodate bakers in different countries and from different cultures, measurements throughout this book have been provided in both U.S. conventional and metric. To keep things simple, measurement conversions have been rounded. See below for the exact conversions, as well as the rounded versions provided throughout this book.

| Spoons | Actual Conversion* | Standard Metric Used |
| --- | --- | --- |
| 1/4 tsp | 1.2 ml | 1 ml |
| ½ tsp | 2.5 ml | 2 ml |
| 1 tsp | 4.9 ml | 5 ml |
| 1 Tbsp | 14.8 ml | 15 ml |

| Cups | Actual Conversion* | Standard Metric Used |
| --- | --- | --- |
| 1/4 cup | 59.1 ml | 50 ml |
| 1/3 cup | 78.9 ml | 75 ml |
| ½ cup | 118.3 ml | 125 ml |
| 2/3 cup | 157.7 ml | 150 ml |
| 3/4 cup | 177.4 ml | 175 ml |
| 1 cup | 236.6 ml | 250 ml |
| 4 cups | 946.4 ml | 1000 ml / 1 liter |

| Ounces (Weight) | Actual Conversion* | Standard Metric Used |
| --- | --- | --- |
| 1 oz | 28.3 grams | 30 grams |
| 2 oz | 56.7 grams | 55 grams |
| 3 oz | 85.0 grams | 85 grams |
| 4 oz | 113.4 grams | 125 grams |
| 5 oz | 141.7 grams | 140 grams |
| 6 oz | 170.1 grams | 170 grams |
| 7 oz | 198.4 grams | 200 grams |
| 8 oz | 226.8 grams | 250 grams |
| 16 oz / 1 lb | 453.6 grams | 500 grams |
| 32 oz / 2 lbs | 907.2 grams | 1000 grams / 1 kilogram |

* Source: Google Calculator

# Resources

This list is for informational purposes only, and does not necessarily constitute an endorsement of any of these companies. We do not receive payment of any kind by these companies for being listed here. It is the readers' responsibility to properly vet any companies they choose to do business with; we are not responsible for any disputes that may arise.

## Ingredients

**Amazon**
www.amazon.ca / www.amazon.com
Gluten-free flours

**Nuts Online**
www.nutsonline.com
Nuts, gluten-free flours, and more.

## Other

**Celebration Generation**
www.celebrationgeneration.com
Food & lifestyle blog, recipes, photos, cookbooks, and inspiration.

# Index

## Marie Porter

Marie Porter is an Autistic polymath, which is just a fancy way of saying that she knows a lot of stuff - and does even more stuff - with a brain that runs on a different operating system than most. Because of that OS, her career has spanned across many facets: She's a trained mixologist, competitive cake artist, professional costumer, and  - last but not least - author. As of 2017, her written works include 7 cookbooks, 6 specialty sewing manuals, and a tornado memoir. Her work has graced magazines and blogs around the world, she has costumed for Olympians and professional wrestlers, has baked for brides, celebrities, and even Klingons. Marie is now proud to share her wealth of multi-disciplinary knowledge and experience with cooks and seamstresses around the world

## Michael Porter

Michael Porter works in medical manufacturing, and is a food and commercial photographer. His work has appeared in local, national, and international magazines, in catalogs, corporate websites, and as well as in many online media outlets. In addition to being an awesome husband and photographer,  Michael is Celebration Generation's "Chief Engineering Officer", responsible for all custom builds, equipment repairs, and warp engine emergencies. After their home was smashed by a tornado, Michael singlehandedly built all of the cabinetry in their new kitchen!  In his 'spare' time, Michael is an avid home brewer, is pursuing a degree in engineering, and is "in training" to become a Canadian.

### Twisted: A Minneapolis Tornado Memoir

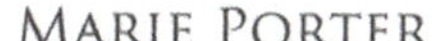
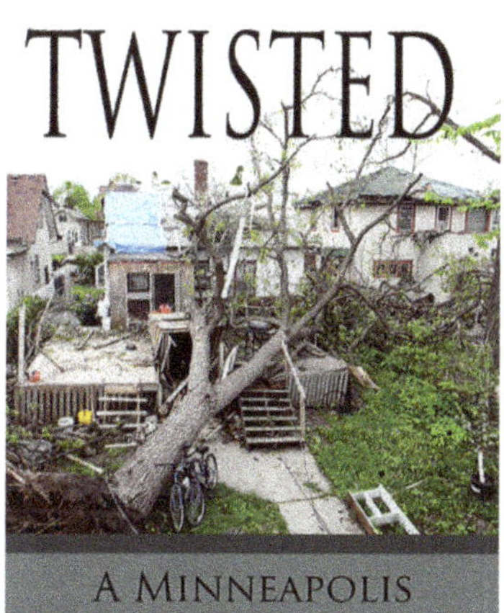


On the afternoon of May 22, 2011, North Minneapolis was devastated by a tornado. Twisted recounts the Porters' first 11 months, post tornado. Rebuilding their house, working around the challenges presented by inadequate insurance coverage. Frustration at repeated bouts of incompetence and greed from their city officials. Dealing with issues such as loss of control, logistics, change, and over-stimulation, as autistic adults. With the help of social media – and the incredibly generous support of the geek community – the Porters were able to emerge from the recovery marathon without too much of a hit to their sanity levels. New friends were made, new skills learned, and a  "new" house emerged from the destruction. Twisted is a roller coaster of emotion, personal observations, rants, humor, social commentary, set backs and triumphs. Oh, and details on how to cook jambalaya for almost 300 people, in the parking lot of a funeral home… should you ever find yourself in the position to do so!

### The Spirited Baker
*Intoxicating Desserts & Potent Potables*

Combining liqueurs with more traditional baking ingredients can yield spectacular results. Try Mango Mojito Upside Down Cake, Candy Apple Flan, Jalapeno Beer Peanut Brittle, Lynchburg Lemonade Cupcakes, Pina Colada Rum Cake, Strawberry Daiquiri Chiffon Pie, and so much more.

To further add to your creative possibilities, the first chapter teaches how to  infuse spirits to make both basic and cream liqueurs, as well as home made flavour extracts! This book contains over 160 easy to make recipes, with variation suggestions to help create hundreds more!

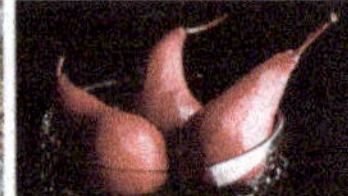

### Evil Cake Overlord
*Ridiculously Delicious Cakes*

Marie Porter has been known for her "ridiculously delicious" moist cakes and tasty, unique flavors since the genesis of her custom cake business. Now, you can have recipes for all of the amazing flavors on her former custom cake menu, as well as many more! Once you have baked your moist work of gastronomic art, fill and frost your cake with any number of tasty possibilities. Milk chocolate cardamom pear, mango mojito.. even our famous Chai cake – the flavor that got us into "Every Day with Rachel Ray" magazine!  Feeling creative? Use our easy to follow recipe to make our yummy fondant. Forget everything you've heard about fondant – ours is made from marshmallows and powdered sugar, and is essentially candy – you can even flavor it to bring a whole new level of "yum!" to every cake you make!

### Beyond Flour
*A Fresh Approach to Gluten-Free Cooking & Baking*

Most gluten-free recipes are developed by taking a "normal" recipe, swapping in a simulated "all purpose" gluten -free flour… whether store bought, or a homemade version. "Beyond Flour" takes a different approach: developing the recipe from scratch. Rather than just swapping out the flour for an "all purpose" mix, Marie Porter uses various alternative flours as individual ingredients – skillfully blending flavours, textures, and other properties unique to each flour – not making use of any kind of all-purpose flour mix. Supporting ingredients and different techniques are also utilized to achieve the perfect end goal … not just a "reasonable facsimile".  With Beyond Flour, you can now indulge in some of your deepest, darkest guilty pleasure  food cravings - safely and joyously!

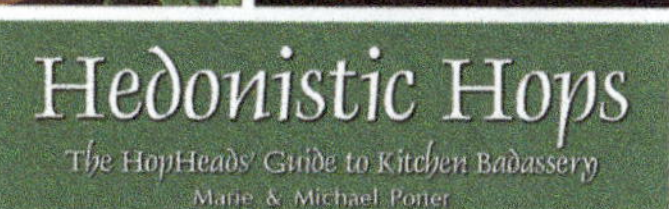

### Hedonistic Hops
*The HopHead's Guide to Kitchen Badassery*

While hops may seem like a bizarre or exotic item to cook with, they're really not that different from any other herb or spice in your cupboard… you just have to know what to do with them! From condiments, sides, & main dishes, to beverages and desserts, Marie Porter creates delicious recipes utilizing hops of various flavour profiles - playing up their unique characteristics - to create recipes full of complex flavour. Much like salt or lemon juice can be added to dishes to perk them up, a small amount of hops - used wisely, and with specific techniques to do so in a balanced fashion - can really make a dish sing. Even those who are not fans of beer will love the unique flavours that various types of hops can bring to their plate. Floral, earthy, peppery, citrusy…Cooking with hops is a great way to expand your seasoning arsenal!

### Beyond Flour 2
*A Fresh Approach to Gluten-Free Cooking & Baking*

How many times have you come across a gluten-free recipe claiming to be "just as good as the normal version!", only to find that the author must have had some skewed memories on what the "normal" version tasted, looked, and/or felt like?

How many times have you felt the need to settle for food with weird after-taste, gummy consistency, or cardboard-like texture, convinced that this is your new lot in life?

Continuing where its predecessor left off, "Beyond Flour 2" is full of tasty gluten-free recipes that have been developed from scratch to be the absolute best they can be - as good or better than the "real" thing - with no "all purpose" mixes, and no need to  compromise on taste or texture!

### More Than Poutine
*Favourite Foods From My Home and Native Land*

With 2017 being Canada's 150th birthday, it was time for me to finally write the Canadian cookbook I'd been planning for YEARS.

So, I did.

"More Than Poutine" is a Canadian cookbook like no other - written by a Canadian living away, it includes recipes for both traditional regional and national homecooked dishes, as well as for accurate homemade replica recipes for many of the snacks, sauces, convenience foods, and other items that are hard to come by, outside of Canada!

High quality gluten-free versions of most recipes are included.

## Introducing Marie Porter's "Spandex Simplified" Series

*Prior to her cake career, Marie Porter had an illustrious \ career in spandex costuming. Now, you can learn all of her secrets to spandex design and sewing!*

Synchro and recreational swimwear, figure skating attire, gymnastics leotards, fitness / bodybuilding posing suits, superheroes, cosplay , and dancewear are all covered in Marie's new Spandex Simplified series, and are all about designing and creating spectacular and durable competitive sports costuming.

These books are appropriate for beginner to advanced levels of sewing ability,and is written from both a designer, and former "performance" athlete's point of view. They teach everything from the basics, to tricks of the trade. The "Spandex Simplified" series will prepare the reader to design and make almost any design of competitive synchro suit, skating dress, or gymnastics leotard imaginable. Given the cost of decent competition suits, these manuals can pay for themselves with savings from just one project!

The books are written completely in laymans' terms and carefully explained, step by step. Only basic sewing knowledge and talent is required. Learn everything from measuring, to easily creating ornate applique designs, to embellishing the finished suit in one book!

*For a complete table of contents listings, current releases, and more info, visit*

## www.spandexsimplified.com

*Wholesale and group purchasing available*